To: EMMA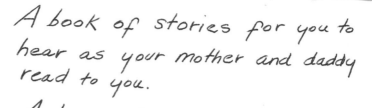

A book of stories for you to hear as your mother and daddy read to you.

A book of stories for you to learn to read yourself so that you can tell the stories to your grandmothers and your cousins.

A book of truth for you to read all the rest of your life.

AT Christmas, 2002 from a far-away friend who thinks you are a bright and gifted young lady.

Linda ELAINE Traylor

MY BIBLE JOURNEY

PRESENTED TO:

Emma

PRESENTED BY:

Linda Traylor

DATE:

Christmas, 2002

Published by World Bible Publishers, Inc., Iowa Falls, Ia 50126

ISBN 0-529-11580-8

Printed in the United States of America

1 2 3 4 5 6 7 – 08 07 06 05 04 03 02

MY BIBLE
JOURNEY

WRITTEN BY MARY HOLLINGSWORTH
ILLUSTRATED BY DENNIS EDWARDS

WORLD
BIBLE PUBLISHERS, INC.
Iowa Falls, IA 50126 U.S.A.

TABLE OF CONTENTS

THE OLD TESTAMENT

NEW TESTAMENT

THE OLD TESTAMENT

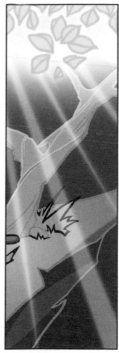

IN THE *Genesis 1–3*
BEGINNING

*G*od! Nothing else existed. The earth was empty. No plants, no animals, no fish, and no people could be found. Land and seas all ran together. Everything was totally dark because no sun, moon, or stars hung in the inky-black void. Houses, streets, and cities had never been built. Computers, airplanes, and cars had not even been imagined yet. Only the great Spirit of God—the wonderful Spirit of love—was alive when time began.

Have you ever wondered where we all came from, and how we got here? Who are we, and where are we going anyway? What are we supposed to do with this time called "life"? What happens after we die? Or can we live forever? Who is God, and how did it all begin?

People have been trying to answer these questions for as long as they have been on earth. And today, we must

Creation	3000–2500 B.C.	2400 B.C.
GOD CREATES THE WORLD	**NOAH AND THE FLOOD**	**THE TOWER OF BABEL**

answer them for ourselves. Here is the story of how it all happened, as told by God himself, because he's the only one who really knows.

THE STORY OF CREATION

In the beginning God created the sky and the earth. And during the next six days, he created everything else in the world and around the world—earth and skies, land and seas, animals, birds, fish, and plants. He made the sun, moon, and stars. And finally, he made people.

• The first great civilization known in the world was the country and people of Sumer. Their influence as a nation was probably at its height during this time.

• The first written language was most likely created by priests in the country of Sumer. They drew pictures on clay tablets with a sharp reed.

• The concept of "zero" in math was probably understood for the first time during this period of time.

• White, painted pottery was probably being made in both Egypt and southeast Europe at this time.

God loved the people he had made most of all. He loved them so much that he wanted them to be like him. He named the first two people Adam and Eve, and he put them in charge of everything else he had made. Then he gave them a beautiful garden for a home. And every night God came and walked in the pretty garden in the cool evening breeze and talked to the people he loved.

A SNAKE IN THE GRASS

One day an evil snake came into the garden. It showed Eve some delicious fruit that grew on the tree in the center of the garden, and it talked her into eating some of the fruit. But God had told Adam and Eve not to eat fruit from

that tree. Eve ate some of it anyway; then she gave some to Adam, and he ate it, too.

God was very sad when the people he loved so much did not obey him. Because he was honest and just, he had to punish Adam and Eve for doing wrong. So he put them out of the garden forever. And they had to work hard to raise their food and make their own clothes. He also punished the snake by making it crawl on its belly in the dirt forever. (That's why snakes don't have legs today! They have to slither instead of run.)

DID YOU KNOW...

that no one really knows exactly when Creation happened? But the first year recorded on the Jewish calendar is 3760 B.C. That's over 5,750 years ago!

THE GREAT
Genesis 6–9
3000–2500 B.C. FLOOD

*A*fter God had to put Adam and Eve out of the Garden of Eden, people became more and more evil. Almost 1,650 years passed after the world had been created. During that time people became so evil that God sadly decided he had to destroy the world he had made. The people he loved had stopped loving him–everyone, that is, except a man named Noah.

Noah was a good man who loved God with all his heart. He and his family obeyed God's commands. The Bible says, "Noah walked with God," just as Adam and Eve had walked with him in the garden before they sinned. So God decided to save Noah's family. He told Noah and his sons to build a huge boat (called an "ark") because he was going to flood the whole world with water and drown every living thing that wasn't on the boat. So Noah and his sons built the boat exactly as God told them.

Creation	3000–2500 B.C.	2400 B.C.
GOD CREATES THE WORLD	NOAH AND THE FLOOD	THE TOWER OF BABEL

BUILDING THE BOAT

The boat was gigantic! In fact, it was longer than a football field and had three stories (called "decks"). It was made out of gopher wood—a special kind of wood God told them to use. And it had a window that ran along under the roof all the way around the top of the boat. It also had one big door where

people, animals, and supplies could be put on the boat.

It took many months for Noah and his sons to build the boat. But it was finally finished. Then God sent a pair of each kind of animal and bird in the world to Noah to be saved from the flood. He sent seven pairs of some special kinds of birds and animals. After the flood was over, these animals and birds would have babies and fill the earth with creayures again.

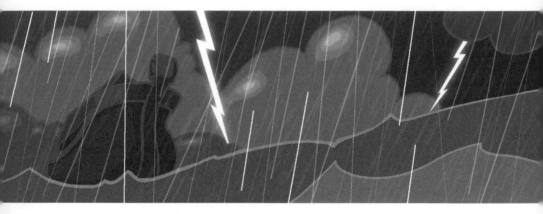

GET ON BOARD!

Noah, his family, and all the animals got on the boat. Then God himself closed the big door. And it started to rain. It rained for forty days and nights! Water also came up from springs in the ground. Finally, the whole world was covered with water, even the mountains were twenty feet under water! Every person,

DID YOU KNOW...

every animal, and every bird that had lived on earth died, except those on the boat with Noah.

The people and animals stayed on the boat for over a year. At long last, the water went away and the land dried out. Then Noah, his family, and God's zoo came off the boat to a brand new world that was clean and good, just as God had created the world the first time. God had taken care of the people he loved and who loved him.

GOD'S PROMISE

Then God made an agreement with Noah. He promised that he would never again destroy the entire earth with a flood, no matter how evil people became. Suddenly the first rainbow

· **2600** B.C. **Yucatan Peninsula.** The Mayan civilization was set up and growing about this time.

· **Sumer.** Pepi's papyrus entitled "Instructions to a Son" was written. This is one of the earliest works of literature that has been saved.

· **Sumer and Egypt.** Schools are set up to teach reading and writing to boys.

· **Egypt.** The great sphinx of Giza was built. The Egyptians thought it guarded the pyramids. It was one of the forms of their false god of the sun. Its face may have looked like Khafre, the king of Egypt.

appeared in the sky. God said the rainbow will appear when it rains, and when he sees it he will remember his agreement not to destroy the entire earth with water. Today, when we see a rainbow, we know that God is taking care of the people he loves and those of us who love him.

WHAT DID YOU SAY?

Genesis 11:1–9
2400 B.C.

*D*id you ever wonder why there are so many different languages in the world? Why can't everyone just speak the same language, and all our problems would be over, right? That's not what God thought.

After God had saved his people from the flood, they began to have children and become a bigger and bigger nation. And, once again, as they grew larger, they forgot about God, his love for them, and how much they needed him. Sin and evil came back into the world, and people no longer obeyed God's commands.

3000–2500 B.C.	2400 B.C.	2091–2066 B.C.
NOAH AND THE FLOOD	THE TOWER OF BABEL	ABRAHAM/ISAAC BORN & SACRIFICED

THE TOWER OF BABEL

As the people moved east, they settled in the Plain of Shinar in Babylon. There they decided to build a great city with a tower so high they said it would "reach the heavens." This meant they didn't feel they needed God anymore. They thought they could reach heaven without his help.

The people also wanted to make a name for themselves or become famous. They thought if they worked together, they could do anything they wanted to do… without God's help.

At that time, all people in the whole world spoke the same language. But God didn't like the way they were thinking. They were too proud of their own abilities and had forgotten him. So he decided to remind people of how much they needed him and to make them depend on him again.

LANGUAGE BECOMES CONFUSED

God went down to the tower, which was probably built like an

ancient ziggurat, and confused the language of the people
building it. In other words, they all started speaking different
languages and couldn't understand each other anymore. When
they could no longer talk to each other, they stopped building
the tower. Then they moved away to different parts of the world
to settle in groups with other people who spoke the same
languages they did.

The city and tower that the people had begun to build was named Babel, which sounds like the Hebrew word for confused. Today, when someone is talking nonsense, we sometimes say, "Oh, stop your babbling."

Anytime we forget that God is in control of our lives, we start babbling, too.

So, when you hear someone speaking a different language than your own, remember that God wants us to depend on him and his grace to get to heaven. We can't get there on our own.

DID YOU KNOW...

the first great libraries were built in Mesopolumia about this same time?

THE NATIONS
Genesis 12–23
2091–2066 B.C. BEGIN

*W*hen the people left Babel and moved to all parts of the world, families got together to form clans, clans formed tribes, and tribes combined to form nations. Each of us descended from one of these great nations.

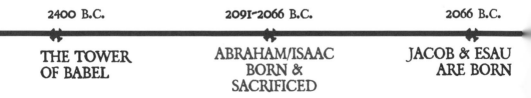

2400 B.C.	2091–2066 B.C.	2066 B.C.
THE TOWER OF BABEL	ABRAHAM/ISAAC BORN & SACRIFICED	JACOB & ESAU ARE BORN

CHOSEN TO SERVE

One nation was made up of Hebrew people, who were descendants of Noah and his son, Shem. The Hebrew nation is talked about in the Bible more than any other nation because God chose it to serve a very special purpose. After Adam and Eve sinned, God put his plan into motion to save his people from their sins and bring them back to him. He planned to send his Son Jesus into the world to save the people he loved so much. But first, he had to prepare the world for Jesus. And he needed a pure nation into which Jesus could be born. He chose the Hebrews to be that nation.

After the Hebrews were chosen by God for this special job, the Old Testament doesn't tell much about the other nations in the world. (The stories of those nations are told in other world history books.) The Bible mostly records the story of the

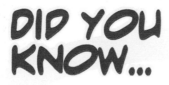

the Hebrews of Abraham's time are the same people we call Jews today?

Hebrew people preparing for Jesus' coming. God used this great family to keep his worship and truth pure. Through them God blessed the whole world with Jesus because he loves us all so deeply.

GOD'S PROMISE

About eight generations after Shem lived, Abram was born in the Hebrew nation. When Abram grew to be a man, God called him to be the father of the Hebrews, and he promised Abram that all the nations of the earth would be blessed through him and his children. Then he changed Abram's name to Abraham, which means "honored father of many."

Abraham and his wife, Sarah, grew very old, but they still had no children. Was God going to keep his promise? Finally, when Abraham was one hundred years old, and Sarah was ninety years old, they had a baby boy named Isaac. At last it seemed that God was keeping his promise to make Abraham the father of a great nation. But one day when Isaac was a young man, God told Abraham to take Isaac and offer his son as a sacrifice to him. Abraham didn't understand why

IN THE WORLD

- **Egypt**. The Pharaohs began ruling as the kings (and one queen) of Egypt.

- **Babylon**. Poems were written celebrating the creation of the world.

- **Egypt**. The Isis and Osiris cult, who believed in the resurrection of the dead, was established.

- **Egypt**. The Saqqara pyramids were built.

- The bow and arrow is known to have been used in warfare.

God asked him to sacrifice Isaac, but he trusted God completely, and he did as God had told him to do. Just as he was about to kill Isaac for the sacrifice, an angel stopped him.

Because Abraham did not keep his only son from God, he was blessed greatly by God and became the father of millions of Hebrew people down through the ages. God always keeps his promises to the people he loves.

TWIN NATIONS ARE BORN

Genesis 25–28
2066 B.C.

*W*hen we think about God's "chosen people," we often think that they were amazing, superhuman people, don't we? We may think they were chosen because they were special people. But the Hebrew nation was full of ordinary people, just like us, who were chosen for a special job.

Sometimes God's chosen people did things the right way; sometimes they made mistakes. Sometimes they worshiped and served God as he asked; sometimes they forgot about God and turned to the false gods of nations around them. They often sinned against God, but then they changed their hearts and lives and came back to him.

Whether the Hebrew people obeyed God perfectly or not, they still had a special job to do. And God, who loved

2091 B.C.	2066 B.C.	1885 B.C.
ABRAHAM/ISAAC–– BORN & SACRIFICED	JACOB & ESAU ARE BORN	THE 12 TRIBES OF ISRAEL/ JOSEPH IN EGYPT

them so much, helped them do it. He was always protecting them, correcting them, and leading them toward their goal of bringing Jesus into the world.

ISAAC, THE NEW LEADER

After Abraham died, his son Isaac became leader of the Hebrew people. Isaac was very much like his father. He did some of the same things well, and he made some of the same mistakes his father had made.

When Isaac was forty years old, he married Rebekah, and they had twin boys named Esau and Jacob. God told Rebekah that her two sons would be leaders of two different nations

some day. He said that when they grew up, the baby born first would serve the baby born second. That meant that Esau's nation would have to serve Jacob's nation. But that seemed strange to Rebekah and Isaac because Hebrew custom said that the son born first should become the family leader after the father died. It was called a birthright. In other words, the oldest son had certain rights because his birth came first.

THE TRADE

Esau was a hunter, and Jacob was a farmer. One day Esau came home from hunting, and he was very hungry. Jacob had been making some stew, so Esau begged Jacob to let him have some of the stew. Jacob offered to trade Esau some stew for his birthright. Esau was so hungry that he didn't act wisely; he agreed to the trade. And that's how God's promise to Rebekah came true. Esau, who was older, had to serve his younger

brother Jacob because Jacob owned the birthright.

Why was that so important? When Isaac died, Jacob, not Esau, became the leader of the Hebrew nation, and it was through that nation—God's chosen people—that Jesus was born into the world. Esau had given up his right to give the world its Savior.

ONE PEOPLE, TWELVE TRIBES

Genesis 29–50
1885 B.C.

*J*ust as God had told Isaac and Rebekah, their younger son Jacob became leader of the Hebrew people after Isaac died. Esau's family, the Edomite nation, often served or fought the Hebrews, as God had said.

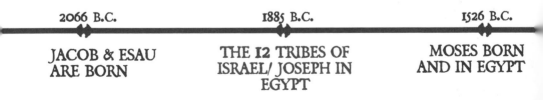

2066 B.C.	1885 B.C.	1526 B.C.
JACOB & ESAU ARE BORN	THE 12 TRIBES OF ISRAEL/ JOSEPH IN EGYPT	MOSES BORN AND IN EGYPT

TRICKED!

During his travels, Jacob visited his uncle Laban, who had two daughters, Leah (the older one) and Rachel. While there, Jacob fell in love with Rachel and offered to work fo Laban seven years in trade for Rachel to become his wife. Laban agreed

to the plan, but when it came time for the wedding, Laban gave Leah to Jacob instead.

When Jacob discovered that he had been tricked, he became upset and went to see Laban, who said that their custom did not allow a younger daughter to marry before the older one. Laban offered to give Rachel to Jacob, too, if he would then work another seven years to pay for her. Because Jacob loved Rachel,

he agreed. So, in all, Jacob worked fourteen years for Rachel.

Through the years, Jacob became the father of twelve sons and one daughter. His twelve sons later became leaders of twelve large tribes within the Hebrew nation. Rachel was the

mother of two of Jacob's sons—Joseph and Benjamin. And because Joseph was Rachel's first son, he was Jacob's favorite.

SOLD INTO SLAVERY

Joseph's brothers were jealous of Jacob's special love for Joseph. So, one day they grabbed Joseph and sold him to a caravan of people going to Egypt. Then they made their father believe that Joseph had been killed by a wild animal.

In Egypt, Joseph was protected and blessed by God. He became popular with the king (pharaoh), and after a few years was given the second

IN THE WORLD

- **Egypt.** Mercury was first discovered and used.

- **India.** Scientists discovered and named four of the basic elements: earth, air, fire, and water.

- **1800 B.C. Babylon.** Medical instruments were first invented and used.

- **Middle East.** Apples were cultivated and eaten.

- **Babylon.** The kings of Babylonia began the custom of shaking hands.

- **China.** The sport of falconry was practiced.

most important job in the country. As God would have it, a famine (when no food grows) happened in Joseph's homeland, and Jacob sent his ten older sons to Egypt to buy food. Because Joseph ruled over the sale of food in Egypt, his brothers had to come to him for the food. When they saw that it was Joseph, they were afraid he would kill them for what they had done to him years before.

GOOD FOR EVIL

Joseph said, "You meant to hurt me. But God turned your evil into good." Then he hugged his brothers and sent them home to bring Jacob, Benjamin, and his whole family to live in Egypt where there was plenty of food and land. Once again God had taken care of the people he loved and who loved him.

DID YOU KNOW...

God helped Joseph tell the king of Egypt what his dream meant? Then Joseph was taken out of prison and made Egypt's prime minister!

(See Genesis 41)

PAUPER, PRINCE & PROPHET

Exodus 1–6 • 1526 B.C.

A few years after Joseph's family moved to Egypt, the King of Egypt died, and a new king began to rule. This new king didn't know Joseph or what he had done for Egypt.

By this time, the people of Jacob (also called Israel), had many children and had become a strong nation. Egypt was filled with them. The new king became afraid that they would leave Egypt, and the Egyptians would no longer have slaves to work for them. So the king made life hard for the people of Israel. Slave masters forced them to make bricks, build cities, and work in the fields. Still, Israel grew stronger.

At last the king commanded that all boy babies born to Israel be drowned in the Nile River. One Hebrew family

1885 B.C.	1526 B.C.	1446 B.C.
THE 12 TRIBES OF ISRAEL/ JOSEPH IN EGYPT	MOSES BORN AND IN EGYPT	GOD DELIVERS ISRAEL FROM EGYPT

had a baby boy named Moses. His mother hid him from the king for three months. Then she made a basket of reeds and tar, put him in it, and placed the basket-bed in the Nile River.

FROM PAUPER TO PRINCE

Soon the king's daughter came to the river to take a bath. She found the tiny basket-boat and looked inside. Baby Moses was crying, and she felt sorry for him. So she adopted him herself, and took him home to the palace. Moses grew up with

the best food, clothes, education, and training. He was a prince of Egypt!

One day Moses saw an Egyptian man beating a Hebrew slave. Moses killed the Egyptian. Then he ran away from Egypt so that the king wouldn't kill him for what he had done. He went to Midian where he lived with a man named Jethro and his family.

FROM PRINCE TO PROPHET

After many years, the King of Egypt died. The people of Israel prayed for God to rescue them from their slavery, and

IN THE WORLD

- **1700 B.C.** The religion of Judaism was begun.

- **Egypt.** A collection of religious documents called The Book of the Dead *was put together to guide the dead on their spiritual journey.*

- **1500–600 B.C. India.** The Hindu religion was begun. This religion worships false gods and is based on the caste system, which ranks people according to their religious practices.

- **Egypt.** The kithara (KITH-uh-ruh) was developed. This wooden instrument is a larger version of the lyre. It is supported by a strap and played by plucking its strings with a pick.

God heard his people's cry for help.

One day Moses saw something very strange. A bush was on fire, but it wasn't burning up. As he stepped closer, he heard a voice say, "Moses." It was the voice of God! God told Moses that he wanted him to go to Egypt and lead his people out of slavery.

Moses tried to talk God out of sending him to Egypt, but God knew that Moses was perfect for the job. God had made sure that Moses grew up in the king's own palace, spoke the Egyptian language, and had all the right training. Finally, Moses agreed to go and rescue God's people, and God promised to help him every step of the way.

DID YOU KNOW...

Moses wrote the first five books of the Bible? They are called "The Pentateuch." The books are Genesis, Exodus, Leviticus, Numbers, and Deuteronomy.

PHARAOHS &
PLAGUES

Exodus 1–12 • *1446* B.C.

From Mt. Sinai (SY-ny), also known as "the mountain of God," where Moses had seen the burning bush, he and his brother Aaron went to the leaders of Israel and told them all that God had said. They showed Israel some powerful miracles God had given them to use in rescuing Israel from Egypt, and the people believed. And when the people heard that God was sad about their troubles, they bowed down and worshiped him.

1526 B.C.	1446 B.C.	1445 B.C.
MOSES BORN AND IN EGYPT	GOD DELIVERS ISRAEL FROM EGYPT	GOD GIVES MOSES THE TEN COMMANDMENTS

FACING OFF WITH PHARAOH

After that, Moses and Aaron went to see the King of Egypt, called Pharaoh. They said, "This is what the Lord, the God of Israel says: 'Let my people go so they may hold a feast for me in the desert.'"

But Pharaoh refused to let them go and sent Moses and Aaron away. Then he ordered the slave masters to make Israel work even harder than before.

So God said to Moses, "Now you will see what I will do to the king of Egypt. I will use my great power against him, and he will let my people go."

Then God caused ten different plagues (disasters) to happen to Egypt, one after the other, in order to force Pharaoh to let the people of

Israel leave their slavery—Water turned to blood, frogs, gnats, flies, cattle disease, boils, hail, locusts and darkness. The plagues hurt the people of Egypt but not the people of Israel, because God loved and protected his own people.

Each time a plague came upon Egypt, Pharaoh would agree to let Israel leave. But when God stopped the plague, then

Pharaoh would not keep his promise, and he wouldn't let Israel go.

PASSOVER

Finally came the tenth plague, and God went through the land of Egypt and killed the oldest son of each Egyptian family, including the son of Pharaoh. But Israel was not harmed because all the people followed God's command to eat a special meal called Passover and to put lamb's blood above their doors. In the Passover meal they ate roasted lamb to honor God because he passed over their homes without killing their children.

Then Pharaoh said to Moses and Aaron, "Get up and leave my

IN THE WORLD

• **Mexico.** The earliest known settlement in Mexico was established. It was called Chiapa de Carzo.

• The Bible Books of Genesis, Exodus, and Numbers were probably written.

• **1600–1450 B.C. Crete.** The false snake goddess was worshiped and known as the "mother goddess." Three snakes wound around her body and headdress. Some people believe the statue was of a queen or a priestess snake handler. This false religious belief may have come from Mesopotamia.

• **Egypt and India.** Leprosy—the name for several different harmful skin diseases—was identified.

people. You and your people may do as you have asked. Go and worship the Lord. And hurry! If you don't, we will all die!"

THE EXODUS

That same night, exactly 430 years after they came to Egypt, the people of Israel left Egypt. About 600,000 men, along with the women and children, left Egypt

together. They took rich gifts of gold and silver with them from their Egyptian neighbors. And they took a large number of sheep, goats, and cattle.

That night, God led his people out of slavery and into freedom. Every year after that the people of Israel celebrated the Passover Feast and remembered how God rescued them from their enemies.

DID YOU KNOW...

some scholars believe that when Israel left Egypt, counting men, women, children, and other people who went with them, about 2,000,000 people escaped!?

AN AGREEMENT WITH GOD

Exodus 13–40 • 1445 B.C.

*W*ith a shout of joy, the people of Israel left Egypt and started out for the Red Sea. They were free! Suddenly Pharaoh panicked. All the slaves had escaped. So he gathered his entire army and chased after Israel. He finally caught up to the people of Israel at the Red Sea.

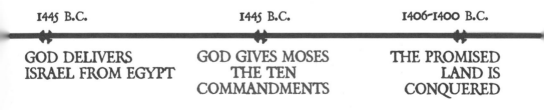

1445 B.C.	1445 B.C.	1406-1400 B.C.
GOD DELIVERS ISRAEL FROM EGYPT	GOD GIVES MOSES THE TEN COMMANDMENTS	THE PROMISED LAND IS CONQUERED

A PATH TO SAFETY

The people of Israel were terrified. Egypt was behind them, and the Red Sea was in front of them. What would they do? Moses told them to stand still and watch the power of God. Moses stretched out his walking stick over the sea, and God made a strong wind blow to form a dry pathway through the sea. Then the people of Israel walked through the Red Sea on dry ground, with a wall of water on each side of them. Amazing! Pharaoh's soldiers tried to follow Israel through the sea, but God caused the water to collapse around them, and they all drowned. God had saved his people again.

IN THE WORLD

- **Egypt**. Fancy tapestries were first made.

- **Egypt**. Harp music was being played for court dances.

- **China**. The first Chinese dictionary was published with over 40,000 characters.

- The Book of Leviticus in the Bible was probably written between 1446-1406 B.C.

- **China**. The famous "Magic Squares" were developed in Chinese mathematics.

- **China**. Silk cloth was being made, which eventually caused increased trade all over the world.

From the Red Sea, Israel traveled about three months to Mt. Sinai, where Moses had first seen the burning bush.

THE AGREEMENT

About 635 years has passed since God promised Abraham that all nations would be blessed through him. But the time had finally come for God to keep his promise. So he came down to Mt. Sinai to renew his Agreement with Abraham's family—Israel.

Until then, everyone had lived under God's law of good versus evil. The other nations would continue living under that law, but God would give Israel a new law—a special law just for them. This law would keep Israel pure and holy, ready to receive God's Son Jesus.

Israel was excited about God's Agreement, but the people didn't know how hard it would be to keep. Moses went up on Mt. Sinai, and the people waited at the foot of the mountain. God wrote ten laws with his own finger onto two stone tablets and gave them to Moses. We call them the Ten Commandments. He also gave Moses over

600 other laws for Israel to follow during the next forty years. We call these the Law of Moses.

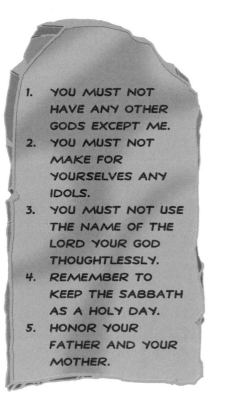

1. YOU MUST NOT HAVE ANY OTHER GODS EXCEPT ME.
2. YOU MUST NOT MAKE FOR YOURSELVES ANY IDOLS.
3. YOU MUST NOT USE THE NAME OF THE LORD YOUR GOD THOUGHTLESSLY.
4. REMEMBER TO KEEP THE SABBATH AS A HOLY DAY.
5. HONOR YOUR FATHER AND YOUR MOTHER.

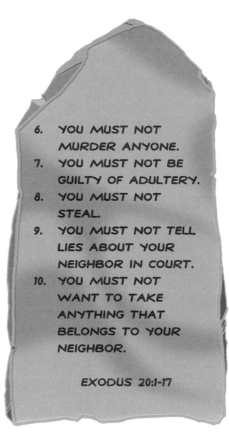

6. YOU MUST NOT MURDER ANYONE.
7. YOU MUST NOT BE GUILTY OF ADULTERY.
8. YOU MUST NOT STEAL.
9. YOU MUST NOT TELL LIES ABOUT YOUR NEIGHBOR IN COURT.
10. YOU MUST NOT WANT TO TAKE ANYTHING THAT BELONGS TO YOUR NEIGHBOR.

EXODUS 20:1-17

Among the laws God gave Moses were directions on how to build a Holy Tent (also called the Tabernacle) for God. The Holy Tent was where God himself would live among the people he loved. It would always be in the center of Israel's camp, just as God should always be at the center of our hearts and lives.

DID YOU KNOW...

God actually wrote the Ten Commandments on stone twice? Moses broke the first stone tablets because the people had made a false god and were worshiping it.
(See Exodus 32:15–20; 34:27–28.)

THE PROMISED LAND

Numbers and
Deuteronomy
1406–1400 B.C.

*T*he Agreement with God had been made, and the
people of Israel promised to keep it. The Holy Tent
had been built, according to God's rules. And Abraham's
family had, at last, become a strong, independent nation.
God had kept his first
promise to Abraham.

Now, it was time for God
to keep his second promise to
Abraham—that his family,
Israel, would be given a
special land in which to live.
It was time for Israel to
march into Canaan—the
Promised Land—and capture
it for their home. So, away
they went toward Canaan.

1445 B.C.	1406–1400 B.C.	1380 B.C.
GOD GIVES MOSES THE TEN COMMANDMENTS	THE PROMISED LAND IS CONQUERED	GOD APPOINTS JUDGES TO RULE ISRAEL

THE GRUMBLERS

Ever since the people of Israel left Egypt, they had been grumbling and complaining to Moses. They complained about the food, the weather, the lack of water, the lack of meat, and all sorts of other things. They often forgot that God had always protected and loved them, and that he would keep on doing so.

When they finally reached the Jordan River, they stopped to prepare for entering Canaan. Moses sent twelve spies—one from each of the twelve tribes—into Canaan to explore the land.

When they returned, ten of the spies

no one knows where Moses was buried? When Moses died, God himself buried Moses, and only he knows where.

(See Deuteronomy 34:5-7)

reported that the people of Canaan were giants and that Israel couldn't defeat them. But two of the spies, Caleb and Joshua, disagreed. They said the land was rich and full of good things to

eat. They believed that with God's help they could defeat Canaan and conquer the Promised Land.

When they heard the reports, the people of Israel were afraid.

They forgot that God was on their side and had promised to give them the victory over their enemies in Canaan. They didn't want to attack Canaan.

ISRAEL IS PUNISHED

God became angry that his people thought they couldn't capture the Promised Land, even with his help. So he punished them by making them wander in the desert for forty long years. He said that none of them over the age of twenty, except for Joshua and Caleb, would be allowed to go into the Promised Land. They would all die in the desert. And that's exactly what happened.

Aaron and Miriam were among the ones who died. And even

Moses was not allowed to go into the Promised Land because he had disobeyed God during the time Israel wandered in the desert. God let Moses look over into Canaan from a mountain, but he could not go in.

A NEW LEADER

Joshua became leader of Israel after Moses died. Under his leadership, and with God at their side, Israel conquered Canaan and received the land God promised to their father Abraham so many years before. It was a beautiful land God had prepared especially for them. In the same way, God has prepared a special land called Heaven for us some day, because we love and obey him. It's a gift God has prepared for the people he loves and who love him.

IN THE WORLD

- **Egypt.** Amenhotep III, a peaceful ruler, was on the throne.

- A large library in the Hittite capital contained stone tablets with writings in eight different languages.

- The Books of Deuteronomy and Joshua in the Bible were probably written.

- **Scandinavia.** Artists began working with bronze.

- **Mediterrania and Scandinavia.** Ship building became much more advanced.

- **Egypt.** Export and import trade greatly increased with countries around the world.

HERE COMES THE JUDGE

Matthew 23–1 B.C.

*J*oshua led the people of Israel in victory over their enemies throughout the Promised Land of Canaan. And yet, Israel did not completely drive out their enemies. That was a big mistake. Over time, the people of Israel settled into their lands and began to farm next to their neighbors who worshiped false gods, such as Baal. And because Baal was thought to rule over farming, Israel's farmers were tempted to worship this false god, too.

1406–1400 B.C.	1380 B.C.	1100 B.C.
THE PROMISED LAND IS CONQUERED	GOD APPOINTS JUDGES TO RULE ISRAEL	RUTH, NAOMI, AND BOAZ

FROM JOSHUA TO JUDGES

When Joshua was 110 years old, he died. He had been a great and faithful leader of God's people, and God had blessed him greatly. After he died, Israel began to forget God once again. When the people forgot him, God allowed their enemies to defeat them. Then they would remember God and call out to him for help. And each time, God heard his people's cries and, because he loved them, would send a leader to rescue them. These leaders were called judges.

For about the next four hundred years, each time the people of Israel changed their hearts and returned to God, he would rescue them. He sent twelve judges in all, one after the other, to save Israel. Here are the names of the twelve judges, in the order they ruled Israel: Othniel, Ehud, Shamgar, Deborah, Gideon, Tola, Jair, Jephthah, Ibzan, Elon, Abdon, and Samson.

JUDGE DEBORAH

All of the judges were men, except for one–Deborah. She was a wise woman, who was respected by the people. She often sat under a huge palm tree known as the Palm of Deborah and held court there. The people of Israel came to her with their problems and complaints, and she helped them solve their problems. Deborah was a brave leader, who led Israel into battle and defeated their enemies. God was with her in whatever she did.

Throughout the time of the judges, Israel seemed to be on a seesaw. Some of the time they worshiped God the way he meant

IN THE WORLD

- **1304** B.C. **Egypt.** Ramses II became king.

- **Egypt.** The people of Israel are first mentioned in an Egyptian victory hymn.

- **1380-1050** B.C. **Canaan.** The Book of Ruth in the Bible was probably written.

- **Mycenae.** The famous Beehive Tomb was found, along with the treasury of Atreus.

- **China.** During the Shang Dynasty, the Chinese people developed high-quality bronze casting. With this process they made the first bells.

- **1350** B.C. **Syria.** The process of welding was invented.

for them to do; other times, they forgot about God and worshiped false gods. When they worshiped God, they were happy and lived well. But when they worshiped false gods, they were unhappy and lived poorly.

In the same way, we will always be happier and live better when our hearts and lives are right with God. When we forget him, we are sad and hurting. God loves us, just as he loved Israel, and he always wants the best for us. If we pray to him when we are in trouble, he will always hear us.

DID YOU KNOW...

the number twelve comes up in the Bible many times. There were twelve sons of Jacob, twelve tribes of Israel, twelve spies into Canaan, twelve judges of Israel, twelve apostles of Christ, and twelve gates into heaven.

A LOVE STORY

Book of Ruth • 1100 B.C.

During the times of the judges in Israel, there was a famine (a time when no food grows) in Israel. Elimelech, his wife, and their two sons moved to the country of Moab where there was food.

After a while, Elimelech died and left his wife, Naomi, with their two sons. When they were old enough, Naomi's two sons married women from Moab. About ten years later, both of Naomi's sons died, leaving Naomi with her two daughters-in-law, Orpah and Ruth.

Soon Naomi heard that God had once again blessed Israel with food, so Naomi, Orpah, and Ruth prepared to go back to Israel. On the way, Naomi told Orpah and Ruth to go back to their own families in Moab where they would be safe and happy. Orpah did as Naomi asked, but Ruth wouldn't leave Naomi. She promised to stay with Naomi always, to become part of her family in Israel, and to worship Naomi's God.

1380 B.C.	1100 B.C.	1090 B.C.
GOD APPOINTS JUDGES TO RULE ISRAEL	RUTH, NAOMI, AND BOAZ	SAMSON IS THE JUDGE IN ISRAEL

RUTH MEETS BOAZ

Ruth went to work in the grain fields in Israel to find food. She first went to the fields of Boaz, one of Naomi's close

IN THE WORLD

- **Assyria.** Tiglath-Pileser founded the Assyrian Empire and conquered Babylon.

- **Mediterranean.** The Phoenicians rose to power. Their cities, Tyre and Sidon, became famous for purple dye, glass, and metal goods.

- **1200 B.C. Babylon.** The poem, The Just Sufferer, showed the people becoming unhappy with their false gods.

- **1200 B.C. Cyprus.** The first enamel work was done by Mycenaeans. Enamel is a metal surface decorated with glass.

- **China.** The sheng mouth organ was developed.

relatives. When Boaz saw Ruth, he was pleased. He had heard how good Ruth was to Naomi, even though Ruth was a Gentile (a person not from Israel). He told his servants to leave extra grain in the field for Ruth.

When a man of Israel died, it was the custom for his closest male relative to buy his land and marry his wife. Naomi thought Boaz was her closest male relative; so she sent Ruth to see him. Boaz said he wanted to buy the land and marry Ruth, but another relative was closer kin to Naomi than he was.

THE BARGAIN

The next day Boaz found the closer relative and asked if he would buy Naomi's land and marry Ruth.

The man said he couldn't do it. Then Boaz said he would buy Naomi's land and marry Ruth.

THE MARRIAGE

Soon Boaz married Ruth, and they had a baby boy

named Obed. Naomi was so excited! She took the baby and helped raise him as if he were her own son. And they lived happily together as a family in Israel.

This love story is important because Obed later became the grandfather of David, King of Israel. And through David's family God's Son, Jesus, was later born into the world. It was all part of God's wonderful plan to save the people he loved.

DID YOU KNOW...

to seal a bargain in Israel, one man took off his sandal and gave it to the other man? In this story Naomi's close relative gave his sandal to Boaz in front of the leaders of the city.

(See Ruth 4:7-12.)

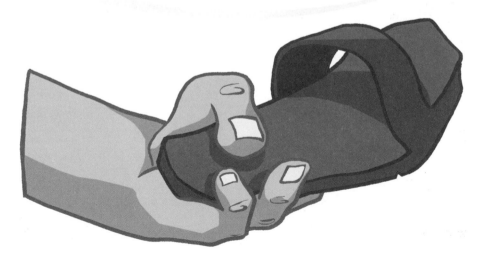

SAMSON: Judges 13–16
1090–1050 B.C.
GOD'S STRONG MAN

*D*uring the later times of the judges, Israel had turned
away from God once again. So, he let the Philistine
people capture Israel. The Philistines kept Israel captive for
forty years.

Then one day an angel of God spoke to the wife of
Manoah, a man from Israel. The angel told Manoah's wife
that she would have a baby and that the baby was to be
given to God's service from the first day he was born. He
was never to cut his hair. He would save Israel from the
power of the Philistines.

When this baby grew up, he became one of the most
interesting and exciting judges of Israel. His name was
Samson, and God made him the strongest man that ever
lived, even until today.

1100 B.C.	1090 B.C.	1043 B.C.
RUTH, NAOMI, AND BOAZ	SAMSON IS THE JUDGE IN ISRAEL	SAUL IS ANNOINTED ISRAEL'S FIRST KING

SAMSON'S SECRET

The secret of Samson's strength was his hair. He promised God he would never cut it. As long as he didn't cut it, he had superhuman strength from God, and he defeated thousands of Philistines. But if he ever cut his hair, he would become as weak as any other man.

DID YOU KNOW...

Samson told this riddle to the Philistines: "Out of the eater comes something to eat. Out of the strong comes something sweet." Can you guess the answers? **(See Judges 14:5-6, 8-9)**

Answers: A lion and honey.

Samson was strong, but he had one big weakness—he liked women too much. One woman he loved was Delilah, but she was a spy for the Philistines. Some Philistine kings offered to pay Delilah a lot of money to find out the secret to Samson's strength.

Several times Delilah asked Samson where his strength came from. Each time he told her a lie. But finally, Samson got tired of Delilah bothering him and told her his secret. Then, while he was sleeping in her lap, she cut off his hair. When he woke up, Samson was as weak as any other man because his promise to God had been broken.

- **1090–945** B.C. **Egypt.** Civil war (Egyptians fighting other Egyptians) was fought while Ramses XI was King of Egypt.

- **Israel.** The Age of the Judges continued.

- **Assur.** Giant tower temples were built for their false gods.

- **1000** B.C. **China.** Ice was being used. They cut ice from frozen lakes during the winter and stored it to chill food in the summer.

- **China.** Prohibition (a law against drinking alcohol) was put into place.

Then the Philistines captured Samson and poked his eyes out. They took him to the city of Gaza, where they put him in bronze chains in prison. But his hair started to grow again.

SAMSON'S REVENGE

Sometime later the Philistine

kings were having a feast for their false god Dagon. They brought Samson in to perform for them. Then they stood him between the huge pillars (posts) that held up the roof to the temple where they were. Samson put his hands out to his sides, one on each of the two huge pillars. Then he prayed that God would give him superhuman strength one more time.

Samson said, "Let me die with the Philistines!" Then, with God's help, he pushed with all his might. The pillars broke apart, and down came the temple on top of Samson and the Philistines. Samson died, but so did thousands of Philistines. God had saved his people again.

SAUL: ISRAEL'S FIRST KING

1 Samuel 1–15 • 1043 B.C.

*T*he last great judge in Israel was a man named Samuel. He was also a great prophet of God. The Promised Land, Canaan, was almost completely under Israel's control. And God knew the time had come when the people of Israel would reject him as their only king. They would want a human king, like the nations around them. So, he sent Samuel to anoint the king he had chosen. The kings would not rule with their own power, but with the power of God.

1090 B.C.	1043 B.C.	1004 B.C.
SAMSON IS THE JUDGE IN ISRAEL	SAUL IS ANNOINTED ISRAEL'S FIRST KING	DAVID BECOMES KING OF ISRAEL

SAUL WAS CHOSEN

God lead a young man named Saul to the city where Samuel was, and Samuel told him that God had selected him to be king over Israel. Saul was surprised because he came from the tribe of Benjamin—the smallest tribe in Israel. But God had prepared Saul to be king. He was a good man, and he was a head taller than anyone else in Israel.

Saul became king when he was thirty years old, and he was King of Israel for forty-two years. He was a brave leader, but he was only a man, so he made some mistakes. His biggest mistake was that he didn't always obey God. This made God sad.

IN THE WORLD

- **North America.** A people known as the Mound-builders were building burial mounds and other large works of dirt.

- **India.** Alexander the Great invaded the country.

- **Israel.** The Age of the Kings was begun.

- **Israel.** David was composing songs, which he played for King Saul. These songs and prayers set to music later became part of the Book of Psalms in the Bible.

- **1000 B.C. India.** Sugarcane was being grown and made into syrup.

- **Phoenicia.** Tin was being imported from mines in England.

SAUL'S SIN

One time Samuel told Saul that God was going to punish the Amalekite people because they had ambushed the Israelites when they were leaving Egypt. God wanted Saul to attack the Amalekites and totally destroy everything that belonged to them.

So, Saul called his army together, and they attacked the city of Amalek. They destroyed everything that belonged to the Amalekites... almost. They took King Agag captive, and they kept some of the things that were good, such as the best sheep and cattle, camels and donkeys. Saul did not obey all of God's command.

Samuel met Saul and told him that God was not happy because Saul had disobeyed him. Then he told Saul that God would not allow Saul's family to be kings of Israel after Saul died. Another family would be appointed as Israel's kings.

SAUL'S INSANITY

As time went by, Saul became jealous and angry because his family would no longer be kings. When Saul's mind became upset thinking about it, a young man named David would calm Saul by playing his harp and singing for him. David and Jonathan, Saul's son, were best friends. But it was David's family that would become kings of Israel in Saul's place. So, the plot of God's story took an interesting turn.

King Saul asked a witch to help him talk to the spirit of Samuel, who had died? And Samuel appeared! But the witch didn't bring him back, God did.

(See 1 Samuel 28:1-19.)

DAVID:
KING, WARRIOR, SINGER

The Book of 2 Samuel
1004 B.C.

*A*s Saul's kingship was ending, David was becoming a most powerful and popular man in Israel. Because he defeated thousands of Israel's enemies, he became a hero. This made King Saul jealous and angry, so he tried to kill David several times. Each time he failed because God was taking care of David, whom he had chosen as

1043 B.C.	1004 B.C.	970-960 B.C.
SAUL IS ANNOINTED ISRAEL'S FIRST KING	DAVID BECOMES KING OF ISRAEL	SOLOMON BUILDS THE TEMPLE OF GOD

the next king to rule over his people.

After several years, Saul and Jonathan were both killed in battle. When David heard about it, he tore his clothes to show how sad he was, and he cried. All of Israel cried. Then David sang a funeral song to honor Saul and Jonathan, which is recorded in 2 Samuel 1:17–27.

DAVID, THE KING

After Saul's death, God sent David to Hebron in Judah where he was appointed king. He ruled as king over Judah for seven years before he became king over all of Israel. David was

thirty years old when he became king, and he ruled for forty years. He was the greatest king that Israel ever had.

Before David became king, the Jebusites had captured the city of Jerusalem, the Holy City of God. And the Ark of the Agreement of the Lord had been removed. The Ark of the Agreement was a special wooden box that held the stone tablets of the Ten Commandments.

David and his armies attacked Jerusalem and defeated the Jebusites. From that time until now, Jerusalem has been also called the City of David. Later, David and the people of Israel found the Ark of the Agreement and brought it back to Jerusalem. As they came into the city, David danced before the Lord, the choirs sang, and the musicians played their flutes, lyres, harps, and trumpets to announce the Ark's arrival. It was a great day for Israel!

DAVID, THE MAN

David tried hard to do everything God told him to do, but sometimes he failed. One time he stole another man's wife and had the man killed in battle. But later, he was very sad for his sin and turned back to God. And that's what made David such a great king and leader of Israel—when he made mistakes, he admitted his wrong

IN THE WORLD

- **Israel**. King Saul died; King David began ruling.

- **Israel**. The earliest known Hebrew inscription dates from this time as the Gezer Calendar.

- **Israel**. The oldest books of the Old Testament were probably put into writing, including the Book of Judges.

- **1000 B.C. Peru**. The people of Peru began worshiping a false god that looked like a cat.

- **Israel**. The Book of Psalms, Israel's Songbook, was being written by King David and a few others.

and came back to the God who loved him so much.

The Bible says that "David was the kind of man God wanted" (1 Samuel 13:14). He wasn't perfect, because no man can be perfect, but he tried his hardest to do what God wanted. That's why God later sent his Son Jesus into the world through David's family.

the Book of Psalms, which contains many songs and prayers written by King David, is the longest book in the Bible?

SOLOMON:
THE WISEST MAN

1 Kings 1–11 • 971–960 B.C.

When David, the "sweet singer of Israel," died, he was buried in the City of David. Right after that, his son Adonijah tried to make himself king. But that was not God's plan, and David's son Solomon was appointed king instead. Right away, Solomon had Adonijah killed. Then Solomon married the daughter of the King of Egypt, in order to stop Egypt from becoming Israel's enemy again. Then Solomon's first few years as King of Israel were peaceful and calm.

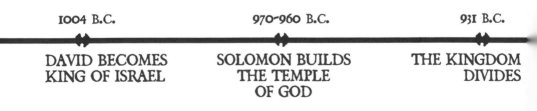

1004 B.C.	970–960 B.C.	931 B.C.
DAVID BECOMES KING OF ISRAEL	SOLOMON BUILDS THE TEMPLE OF GOD	THE KINGDOM DIVIDES

SOLOMON'S WISDOM

One night God spoke to King Solomon in a dream. God said, "Ask for anything you want. I will give it to you." And Solomon said, "I ask that you give me wisdom. Then I can rule your people in the right way." God was pleased with Solomon's

IN THE WORLD

- **Israel.** The Temple to Yahweh (God) was built by Solomon in Jerusalem, and Israel reached the height of its civilization.

- **Israel.** The Bible Books of Proverbs, Song of Songs, and Ecclesiastes were probably written.

- **China.** Brush-and-ink paintings were done.

- **Israel.** Professional musicians performed at religious ceremonies.

- **Mediterranean.** Fabric dyes were made from purple snails.

- **Egypt and Assyria.** Wigs were worn by wealthy people.

answer. So he made Solomon the wisest man who ever lived, both then and now. He also gave Solomon great riches and honor. During his time, there was no other king as great as Solomon.

SOLOMON'S TEMPLE

King David had wanted to build a great temple for God in Jerusalem, but God did not allow David to build it. So, about four years after Solomon became king, he took the plans his father had drawn and built the temple just as the Lord wanted it.

This amazing temple was the most beautiful temple ever built. And it took over seven years to build it. The temple meant that God was still living among his people, just as he had lived in the Holy Tent when they were traveling in the desert after they left Egypt.

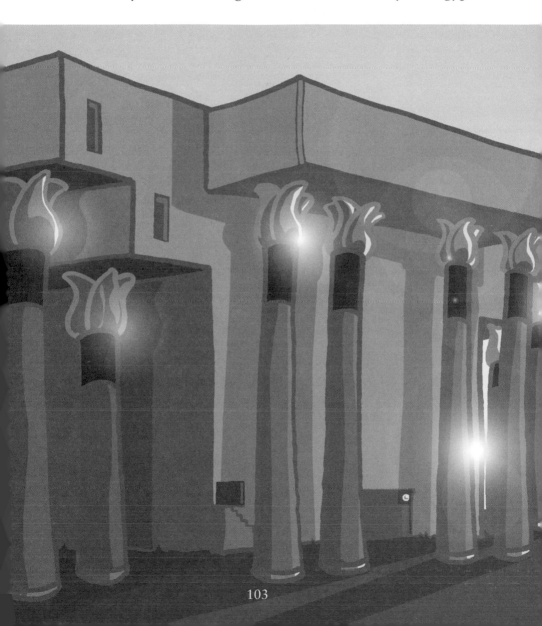

SOLOMON'S FAME

Just as he had promised, God gave Solomon great wisdom, amazing riches, and the highest honor possible. His kingdom was the most peaceful and wealthy that had ever been known. He was so famous that the Queen of Sheba traveled over 1,200 miles by camel through the desert to see if what she had heard about King Solomon was really true. After she saw Solomon and his kingdom, she said, "I was not told even half of it! Your wisdom and wealth are much greater than I had heard."

SOLOMON'S WRITINGS

Because Solomon was so wise, he wrote wise sayings and songs to teach the people about God and life. The wise sayings are called "proverbs." The Bible books of Proverbs, Ecclesiastes, and Song of Songs, as well as some of the Psalms, are all thought to be written by Solomon.

DID YOU KNOW...

Solomon had over 700 wives? He married them to keep peace with the nations around Israel.

DIVIDED!

1 Kings 12–22 & 2 Chronicles • 931 B.C.

Near the end of King Solomon's reign, he thought back over his life. He had lived with great riches, honor from other nations, a powerful kingdom, and worldwide fame—everything most people want. But those things were not worth anything to him compared to living with God forever. His final writings are called Ecclesiastes, and you can read them in your Bible.

971-960 B.C.	931 B.C.	870 B.C.
SOLOMON BUILDS THE TEMPLE OF GOD	THE KINGDOM DIVIDES	ELIJAH CHALLENGES PROPHETS OF BAAL

THE KINGDOM DIVIDES

When Solomon died, his son Rehoboam became king. But Israel was not happy with him as their king because he was mean and unfair to them. He was not wise as his father Solomon had been. So, ten of the twelve tribes of Israel refused to follow Rehoboam, and they chose a new king named Jeroboam. These ten tribes continued to be known as "Israel." But Jeroboam quickly led them to worship false gods, and they turned away from the God who had always loved them and saved them from their enemies.

The other two tribes, Judah and Benjamin, stayed with Rehoboam as their

- **931 B.C. Israel.** The nation of Israel divided into Israel and Judah.

- **922 B.C.** Civil war began between Israel and Judah.

- **Israel.** The Song of Deborah was written.

- **930 B.C. Israel.** The Bible Books of 1 Samuel and 2 Samuel were probably written.

- Egypt conquered Jerusalem—the Holy City.

- **Greece.** Geometric designs were being used on Greek works of art.

- **Northern Europe.** Gold vessels and jewelry were being made and used.

king and became known as "Judah." It was this smaller group of Hebrew people who remained faithful to God most of the time. Because of this, the Levites (those appointed as priests for the Hebrew people) and other good people in Israel who wanted to follow God moved south to join with Judah.

THE TWO KINGDOMS

For the next 100 years, Judah had good kings, like Asa and his son Jehoshaphat, who followed God's law and kept the people faithful to him. Here's what the Bible says about Asa: "Asa did what the Lord said was good and right. He removed the foreign altars used for idol worship. He removed the places

where false gods were worshiped. He smashed the stone pillars that honored false gods… Asa commanded the people of Judah to obey… the Lord's teachings and commandments" (2 Chronicles 14:2–4).

But Israel had seven evil kings in a row, who led them to

worship false gods. So, the two kingdoms of God's people fought with each other and the nations around them.

The kingdom of God was divided, and it would never be united again, until Jesus was born hundreds of years later. It was a very sad time for God's people.

DID YOU KNOW...

the Bible says "Do not be afraid" 365 times? That's once for every day of the year. We should never be afraid with God on our side. Israel forgot that.

(See Luke 1:30)

THE DUEL: GOD VS. BAAL

1 Kings 17–18 • 870 B.C.

*D*uring the years that God's people were divided into the two kingdoms of Israel and Judah, God kept on loving them. Even though they didn't love and obey him, he kept on loving them. When the two kingdoms were not following him, God knew they were like lost children who didn't know which way to go. So, he sent great men of faith to show them the way back to him. The men were called prophets. They brought messages from God to his people.

931 B.C.	870 B.C.	852 B.C.
THE KINGDOM DIVIDES	ELIJAH CHALLENGES PROPHETS OF BAAL	ELISHA THE PROPHET

112

ELIJAH'S MESSAGE

One of the greatest of all prophets to Israel was Elijah. God sent him to speak out against King Ahab and his wife, Jezebel. Elijah told them that, because of their evil ways in worshiping the false god Baal, it would not rain again until he said it would. Right away, the rain stopped, and it didn't rain again in Israel for three years!

Finally, God sent Elijah back to Ahab. He told Ahab to bring all the people of Israel, the 450 prophets of Baal, and the 400 prophets of Asherah (another false god), to Mount Carmel to meet him.

THE DUEL

On the mountain Elijah challenged Israel and the prophets of Baal to a duel. He said, "If the Lord is the true God, follow him.

But if Baal is the true God, follow him" (1 Kings 18:21)! He said the prophets of Baal would prepare one sacrifice, and he would prepare another. Then they would call on Baal, and he would call on God. Whichever god answered the prayers and burned up the sacrifice would be the true God. And the people agreed that it was a good plan.

The prophets of Baal went first. They called on their false god from morning until night. They danced around their altar, and they even cut themselves with swords to show how sincere they were. But Baal did not answer. Nothing happened.

Then it was Elijah's turn. He prepared the sacrifice as God commanded. To prove his point, he had twelve huge stone jars of water poured over the sacrifice. Then Elijah prayed to God to rain down fire from heaven to show the people that he was the one and only true God.

Suddenly, fire from heaven fell on the altar. It burned up the sacrifice. It burned up the altar.

IN THE WORLD

- **Israel.** The city of Samaria was rebuilt as capital of Israel, the northern kingdom.

- **Cyprus.** The people of Phoenicia settled on the island.

- **870 B.C. Israel.** King Ahab married the princess of Phoenicia, Jezebel. They were two of the most evil people ever to live.

- **Greece.** Homer wrote the two long, epic poems called *Iliad* and *Odyssey*.

- **Israel.** The Age of the Prophets began.

- **Assyria.** The royal palace and temple to the false god Ishtar were rebuilt in the city of Ninevah.

And it even licked up the water. Then the people of Israel fell down on the ground and bowed facedown before the Lord. They shouted, "The Lord—he is God!"

Then Elijah had all the false prophets killed. God had won the duel! Elijah did many other amazing works, too, with the Lord's help. Many of his mighty works were like the miracles Jesus did so many years later.

DID YOU KNOW...

while Elijah was hiding from King Ahab, God sent ravens to feed him with bread and meat every day?

(See 1 Kings 17:1–6.)

A WHIRLWIND & A SPECIAL COAT

2 Kings 2–13 • 856 B.C.

*D*uring the time that Elijah was a messenger for God, a young man named Elisha was his helper. Elisha followed Elijah around the country, watching him, talking to him, and learning how to be a prophet himself. Finally, it came time for God to take Elijah out of the world, and Elisha was going to become God's prophet in Elijah's place.

On that special day, Elijah and Elisha were traveling together. They both knew that God was going to take Elijah to heaven that day. They traveled through several towns; then they went to the Jordan River. Elijah took off his coat, rolled it up, and struck the water in the river. Then the river parted, and Elijah and Elisha walked through the river on dry ground to the other side.

Elijah said to Elisha, "What can I do for you before I am taken from you?"

Elisha said, "Leave me a double share of your spirit."

870 B.C.	852 B.C.	755 B.C.
ELIJAH & PROPHETS OF BAAL	ELISHA THE PROPHET	JONAH & THE BIG FISH

He was asking for Elijah's power as a prophet to become his own.

Elijah said, "You have asked a hard thing. But if you see me when I am taken from you, it will be yours. If you don't, it won't happen."

THE WHIRLWIND

As they walked on, suddenly a chariot and horses made of fire appeared. It came between Elijah and Elisha. Then Elijah was taken up to heaven by God in a whirlwind. And Elisha saw it happen. That was the last time Elisha saw Elijah; so Elisha tore his clothes to show how sad he was.

THE SPECIAL COAT

Elisha picked up Elijah's coat that had fallen from him and went back to the Jordan River. He rolled up the coat and hit the water with Elijah's coat, and the river parted just as it had for Elijah. Then Elisha walked through the river on dry ground again.

A group of prophets from Jericho were watching. They said, "Elisha now has the spirit Elijah had." And they bowed down before him.

ELISHA, THE PROPHET

Like his teacher Elijah, Elisha did many mighty works and miracles while he served God as a messenger to Israel.

And, like Elijah, Elisha's miracles were very much like the miracles that Jesus would do when he came years later.

the iron head of an ax once floated on water? God helped Elisha make it float.

(See 2 Kings 6:1-7.)

IN THE WORLD

• **842 B.C. Israel.** Jehu takes the kingship away from Ahab's family.

• **Corinth.** The Dorian people conquer the city of Corinth.

• Leather scrolls replaced clay tablets for writing purposes.

• **Eastern Mediterranean.** Most countries in this region were worshiping false gods, such as winged animals or the sun.

• **Balawat.** Highly developed metal and stone sculptures were being made.

• **China.** Their history was first recorded in date order.

A BIG FISH STORY

The Book of Jonah • 775 B.C.

*D*uring the next sixty years after Elisha's death, the kingdoms of Israel and Judah continued to ignore God and worship idols. And God, who still loved them, sent more of his prophets to warn them to come back to him. He sent Jonah, Hosea, Joel, and Amos to different places with messages for the people. The story of Jonah is one of the most amazing ones.

852 B.C.	755 B.C.	740 B.C.
ELISHA THE PROPHET	JONAH & THE BIG FISH	ISAIAH THE PROPHET

GOD SENT JONAH

One day God told Jonah to go to the huge city of Nineveh to preach against it. Nineveh was the capital city of the Assyrian people, who didn't worship God. The kings of Assyria lived there, and it was an evil city.

Jonah didn't want to go to Nineveh, so he ran away from God. He went down to Joppa and got on a ship going to Tarshish. But God made a great wind blow on the sea, and the waves became very high. The ship was about to break apart! And the sailors were afraid. They started throwing things off the ship to make it lighter

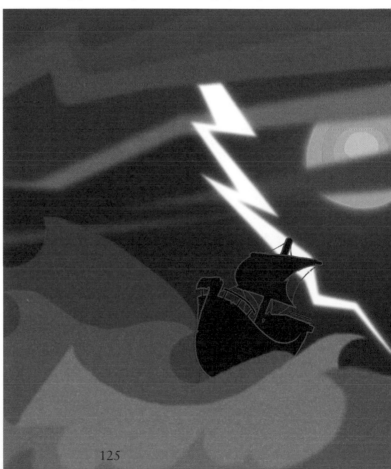

IN THE WORLD

- **Spain.** The Greek people began to settle in parts of Spain.

- **Egypt.** A famous fable was written called The Battle Between Head and Belly.

- **Israel.** The Bible Books of Jonah, Amos, and Joel were probably written.

- **Greece.** The false god Apollo was worshiped at Delphi.

- **Asia Minor.** Arts and crafts were popular, including metal sculpture, carpet weaving, embroidery, and rock carving.

- **Babylonia.** Both the five-tone and the seven-tone musical scales were in use.

so it wouldn't sink. But they were still in danger.

Then the sailors threw lots (something like rolling dice) to see who had caused the storm. The lots showed that it was Jonah's fault. So Jonah told them what he had done. The men tried hard to row the ship to shore, but the storm got stronger and stronger. Finally, they did as Jonah told them—they threw Jonah into the sea.

THE BIG FISH

Then God caused a very big fish to swallow Jonah. He was in the stomach of the fish for three days and three nights. And while he was there, Jonah prayed to God to save him. After that, God made the fish spit Jonah out onto the shore. Then he told Jonah again to go to Nineveh and preach against it. This time,

Jonah did what God said to do. He went to Nineveh.

When the people of Nineveh heard the message Jonah brought to them from God, they believed him. They stopped eating and wore rough cloth called "sackcloth" to show how sad they were for their sins. Everyone in the city did this—poor people, rich people, and even the king.

When God saw that all the people of Nineveh stopped doing

evil things and believed in him, he changed his mind and did not punish them. God is always happy when his people come back to him.

Later, when Jesus came, the Bible compared Jesus' being in the grave for three days to Jonah's being inside the great fish for three days. So the story of Jonah was a clue about what would happen some day.

DID YOU KNOW...

archaeologists have now found the royal library of King Ashurbanipal, who lived in Nineveh? The library contained over 25,000 clay tablets of writing!

ISAIAH: THE JESUS PROPHET

Isaiah 1–17 • 740 B.C.

Jonah was a prophet of God while Jeroboam II was King of Israel. During that same time, Uzziah was King of Judah. While Jonah, Amos, Hosea, and Joel took messages to Israel and Assyria, a prophet named Isaiah was God's messenger to Judah. Isaiah may have been the most powerful of all of God's prophets, and he spoke for God for forty years.

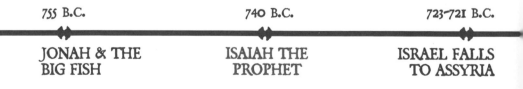

755 B.C.	740 B.C.	723-721 B.C.
JONAH & THE BIG FISH	ISAIAH THE PROPHET	ISRAEL FALLS TO ASSYRIA

THE JESUS PROPHET

Isaiah's message from God was that the people of Judah should repent of their terrible sins before it was too late. He warned them that they would soon be taken captive by Assyria because they continued to sin against God by worshiping false gods. Isaiah described the

IN THE WORLD

- **753 B.C. Italy.** The city of Rome was founded by Romulus and Remus.

- **Israel & Judah.** Prophets Amos, Hosea, Joel, and Isaiah fought religious and social abuses.

- **Israel.** Collecting of *The Sayings of Solomon* was begun.

- **Egypt, Phoenicia, Samaria.** Ivory carving practiced.

- **Mesopotamia.** A system of musical notation was developed, and the earliest hymn was written down.

- **India.** Medical training was done using actual models of the human body.

"terrible day of the Lord" when all the people on earth would be judged guilty by God, just as Israel and Judah were being judged by God.

At the same time, Isaiah often talked with excitement about "the coming Messiah." Messiah means "savior." So, Isaiah was telling Judah about the coming of Jesus, the Savior who would save the people of Judah and Israel from their sins. That's why Isaiah is sometimes called "the Messianic prophet."

Some of God's messages through Isaiah tell what will happen in the future. Even though it was 700 years before Jesus would be born, Isaiah told the people of Judah that Jesus would be called "Immanuel" when he was born. He also told them that the Messiah (Jesus) would be a descendant of King David and that he would set up a kingdom of the

few Hebrew people who still loved and obeyed God. He said that when Jesus came, he would bring peace, justice, and joy.

GOD'S MESSAGE TO THE NATIONS

Although the people of Judah were not faithful to God, he still loved them, and he knew they were part of his ongoing plan to bring Jesus into the world. Because Judah sinned against him, God allowed other nations to take them captive as punishment for their sins. And yet, God would also punish those nations someday for acting against Judah, the people he loved. So, God sent Isaiah to deliver messages of warning to those nations, too.

DID YOU KNOW...

the name Immanuel means "God with us"? Just as God lived among the Hebrews in the Holy Tent and then in the Temple, he was planning to live among his people as Jesus someday.

HOPE FROM HEZEKIAH

At long last, a new king began to rule Judah. His name was Hezekiah, and he loved the Lord. During his reign, Hezekiah repaired the temple of God and returned Judah's worship to him. He even sent an invitation to the kingdom of Israel to join Judah for the annual Passover Feast. And he made many other changes to return Judah to God.

Still, God had shown Isaiah that Judah would not remain faithful to him. So Isaiah warned the people of Judah to keep doing what was right and not to go back to their sinful ways again. If they did, God said they would be taken captive by their enemies, the Assyrians.

CAPTURED!

Isaiah 18–38 • 723–721 B.C.

*C*hange your hearts and lives. Return to God, or you will be taken captive by Assyria! That's what God's prophets had been telling the northern tribes of Israel. But the people of Israel didn't listen, and before long they were taken captive by the Assyrians. Their homes and lands were soon stolen by people from Babylonia and other countries to the east.

Meanwhile, the two tribes of Judah were still standing against Assyria, but probably not for long. So Judah began to ask their neighbor nations for help. One of the nations they turned to was their old enemy, Egypt, with their armies of horses and chariots.

740 B.C.	723-721 B.C.	701 B.C.
ISAIAH THE PROPHET	ISRAEL FALLS TO ASSYRIA	SENNACHERIB INVADES JUDAH

THE NAKED TRUTH

Isaiah then spoke God's message against Egypt and Cush. He was upset because Judah was depending on horses and chariots for help, rather than the power of God. So that people would notice him and listen to God's message, Isaiah—because God said to—went around naked for three years. (The word "naked" in the Hebrew language may have meant that he only took off his outside clothes. But even that was terrible!)

LIVE LONG
AND PROSPER

When it came time for good King Hezekiah of Judah to die, God sent Isaiah to tell him. Isaiah said, "This is what the Lord says: You are going to die. So you should give your last orders to everyone. You will not get well."

When he heard this, Hezekiah turned his face toward the wall and prayed that God would let him live a while longer. Then he cried loudly.

Before Isaiah left Hezekiah's palace, God told him to go back

and speak to Hezekiah again. So Isaiah went back and said, "This is what the Lord said: I have heard your prayer. And I have seen your tears. So I will heal you. Three days from now you will go up to the Temple of the Lord. I will add fifteen years to your life. I will save you and this city from the king of Assyria."

To show Hezekiah that what he had said was true, and that Hezekiah would live another fifteen years, God made the shadow on the stairs go backward ten steps. That's how Hezekiah knew that God could make time go backward in his own life, too. God is awesome—he can do anything!

DID YOU KNOW...

the Assyrian people laughed at King Hezekiah for depending on God? But guess who later got the last laugh!

IN THE WORLD

- **732** B.C. **Israel.** The Assyrian king, Tiglath-Pileser III captured the city of Damascus and made Israel a servant state.

- **Babylon.** The Assyrians seized the throne of Babylon.

- **China.** Peking became the capital of the Yen Kingdom.

- **700** B.C. **Greece.** The poetry of Hessiod, a former shepherd, became popular. His epic poem, Works and Plays, described everyday life in a Greek village.

- The Bible Books of Hosea and Micah were probably written.

- **Babylonia, China.** Astronomers first understood how planets move in their orbits.

GOD SAVES JUDAH AGAIN

Isaiah 39–66 • 701 B.C.

*B*efore King Hezekiah of Judah almost died, Assyria had conquered most of the strong, walled cities of Judah. So Hezekiah sent a message to the King of Assyria whose name was Sennacherib. He asked Sennacherib to leave Judah alone, and he would pay Sennacherib any amount of money he wanted. Sennacherib demanded about 22,000 pounds of silver and 2,000 pounds of gold! But Hezekiah paid Sennacherib what he had asked. Then Sennacherib left… but not for long.

723-721 B.C.	701 B.C.	639 B.C.
ISRAEL FALLS TO ASSYRIA	SENNACHERIB INVADES JUDAH	JOSIAH, YOUNG KING OF JUDAH

HERE THEY CAME AGAIN

Soon Sennacherib's armies attacked Judah's strong, walled cities again, thinking they would capture them for themselves. When Hezekiah heard that Assyria was attacking them again, he worked hard to protect the city of Jerusalem. He and the people repaired the city walls and built another wall around the outside of that. He had towers built on the walls, and he gathered his

armies together ready to fight.

Then Hezekiah went to the Temple and prayed to God: "Lord our God, save us from the king's power. Then all the kingdoms of the earth will know that you, Lord, are

IN THE WORLD

· **681 B.C. Assyria.** King Sennacherib was murdered by two of his three sons in Nineveh. His third son, Essarhaddon, became king in his place.

· **660 B.C. Turkey.** The city of Istanbul was founded. Then it was called Byzantium.

· **660 B.C. Japan.** According to legend, the country of Japan was founded by Jimmu.

· **Judah.** The Book of Isaiah in the Bible was written.

· **Greece.** The false gods Apollo and Dionysus became more popular.

· **700 B.C. Scythia, Europe.** Saddles for horses were invented by the Scythians.

the only God." Later Isaiah came and told Hezekiah that God had heard his prayer, and that he would save Jerusalem from Assyria, just as he had promised before.

That night more than 185,000 of Sennacherib's soldiers died. When the Assyrian people got up the next morning, they found all those dead bodies! So Sennacherib left Jerusalem and went back to Nineveh. God had kept his promise to Hezekiah. He had defended Jerusalem against the Assyrians.

After the fifteen years passed that God gave to Hezekiah, Hezekiah died, and his son Manasseh became king at age twelve. But Manasseh was not faithful to God as his father had been. He led Judah back to the worship of false gods.

ISAIAH'S COMFORT

During his later years, Isaiah's message from God changed.
Most of the ten tribes of Israel were living as captives in foreign

countries. And Judah would be captured before long. With God's help, Isaiah looked ahead in time and saw when Jesus the Messiah would come to set up his kingdom that would last forever. Then Israel and Judah would be rescued, reunited as one nation, and given a place of peace and joy. It would be a wonderful time for the people God loved and who loved him.

DID YOU KNOW...

when someone broke one of the laws of Assyria they were often punished by having their ears cut off? It paid to listen carefully to the law! It still does.

JOSIAH: 2 Kings 21–23
2 Chronicles 33: 1–20
639 B.C.
THE BOY KING

*L*ed by King Manasseh, Judah was once again
worshiping false gods and ignoring the true God of
heaven. So God brought the army of Assyria to attack
Judah again to turn the people back to him. Assyria took
Manasseh captive. The Assyrians put a hook in his nose,
bronze chains on his hands, and they led him away
to Babylon.

There Manasseh prayed to God for help, because he was
very sorry for what he had done. God heard Manasseh's
prayer and felt sorry for him. So he returned Manasseh to
his kingdom in Jerusalem. Then Manasseh knew that God
is the Lord, and he tried to lead Judah back to God. He
tore down the false gods and destroyed their temples. Then
he commanded the people of Judah to worship the
true God.

701 B.C.	639 B.C.	626 B.C.
SENNACHERIB INVADES JUDAH	JOSIAH, YOUNG KING OF JUDAH	JEREMIAH CRIES

NAHUM, THE PROPHET

While Manasseh was helping Judah return to worshiping God, a prophet named Nahum was sent by God with a message against Assyria. At this time Assyria had a cruel and evil king named Ashurbanipal. Nahum went to the city of Nineveh, where Jonah had been about a hundred years before, to tell the people that their city would be destroyed because of their cruelty and evil ways. His message came true in about forty years when Nineveh was completely destroyed.

THE BOY KING

About that same time, King Manasseh died. His son Amon ruled Judah for about two years. Then Amon's son, Josiah, became King of Judah. He was only eight years old when he became king, but Josiah was the best king Judah had ever had. He always did what God said was right.

When Josiah was sixteen years old, he began to make big changes in Judah. He removed the false gods from Judah and Jerusalem. He destroyed the

IN THE WORLD

• **690–638** B.C. **Judah.** Manasseh was King of Judah. He actively supported cult worship, set up Mesopotamian false gods in the Temple of Yahweh in Jerusalem, and practiced child sacrifices.

• **Macedonia.** The Macedonian kingdom was set up.

• **Judah.** The Book of Nahum in the Bible was probably written.

• **650** B.C. Leprosy, a group of harmful skin diseases, was first identified. There is still no complete cure today.

• **624** B.C. **Greece.** Horse racing was added to the Olympic Games.

places for worshiping false gods. He removed the Asherah idols, the wooden and metal idols, and the Baal gods. Then Josiah cut down the incense altars above the idols. He broke up the Asherah idols and the wooden and metal idols. He beat them into powder and sprinkled the powder on the graves of the people who had worshiped those false gods. He burned the bones of their priests on their own altars.

Finally, young King Josiah made the Temple of God in Jerusalem pure again. And he led his people—the people God loved—back to devotion and worship of the one true God of heaven. Josiah was, without a doubt, the greatest king Judah ever had.

He was a man like his ancestor, King David, who was the kind of man God wanted.

DID YOU KNOW...

the Assyrians were so cruel and evil during this time that they would boil their enemies in oil or skin them alive?

JEREMIAH: THE PROPET WHO CRIES

The Book of Jeremiah • 626 B.C.

*D*uring the thirteenth year that King Josiah ruled Judah, God chose another prophet to take his message to them. Like Josiah, this prophet was just a young man when God chose him to be his special messenger. His name was Jeremiah, and he belonged to the family of priests who lived in a small village called Anathoth. Their village was in the land where the tribe of Benjamin had settled.

639 B.C.	626 B.C.	621 B.C.
JOSIAH, YOUNG KING OF JUDAH	JEREMIAH CRIES	JOSIAH FINDS THE BOOK OF THE LAW

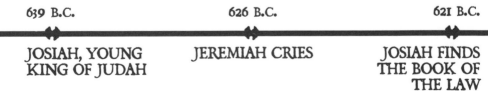

GOD CALLS JEREMIAH

God said to Jeremiah, "Before I made you in your mother's womb, I chose you. Before you were born, I set you apart for a special work. I appointed you as a prophet to the nations."

But Jeremiah said to God, "But Lord God, I don't know how to speak. I am only a boy."

Then God said, "Don't say, 'I am only a boy.' You must go everywhere that I send you. You must say everything I tell you to say. Don't be afraid of anyone, because I am with you. I will protect you." Then God reached out and touched Jeremiah's mouth and said, "See, I am putting my words in your mouth."

IN THE WORLD

- **Babylon.** The Assyrians destroyed Babylon and changed the course of the Euphrates River until it covered the city of Babylon with water.

- **Sicily.** Ballads about great heroes were being written by Stesichorus.

- **Judah.** The Bible Books of Jeremiah and Zephaniah were probably written.

- **630–553 B.C. Persia.** Zoroaster began a new, one-god religion that worshiped the false god Ahura-Mazda.

- Kaleus was the first to sail a ship through the Straits of Gibraltar.

- **Greece.** Ornamental weaving was being done.

JEREMIAH'S TWO DREAMS

God gave Jeremiah two dreams. In the first dream Jeremiah saw a stick of almond wood. And God said, "This means that I am watching to make sure my words come true." (The Hebrew word for "watching" sounds like the Hebrew word for "almond tree.")

In the second dream Jeremiah saw a pot of boiling water that

was tipping over from the north. To the people of Jeremiah's time, a boiling pot stood for war. Then God explained that the pot of boiling water meant that disaster would come to Judah from the north.

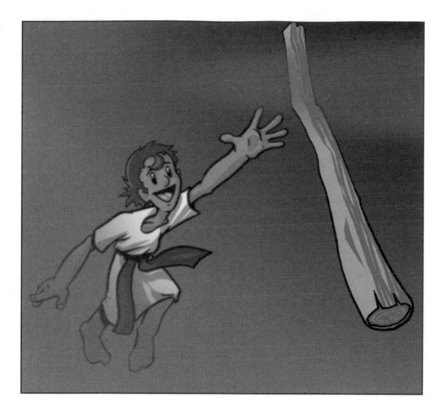

JEREMIAH'S TROUBLES

For the next fifty years, Jeremiah spoke God's message against Judah and Jerusalem. All the other priests were wrongly saying they were going to have peace. So the people chose not to believe Jeremiah. They didn't want to hear his warning about the war and trouble. They treated Jeremiah cruelly. And they stood up against him and his message—the warning from God.

During this time the strong nations around them were at war. Assyria, Babylonia, and Egypt were all fighting each other. After several years, Babylon and their ruler, King Nebuchadnezzar, were the winners. Sadly for Judah, it was Babylon that would be the boiling pot of water in Jeremiah's dream. Babylon would come down from the north and take Judah captive.

GOOD NEWS

Most of Jeremiah's message to Judah was sad, but you can read happy news in his words, too. Through Jeremiah God said that he was going to make a new agreement with Judah and Israel. He said he would forgive their sins and put his new law in their hearts. God was telling his people the good news about the time when Jesus would come to save them!

Jeremiah is called the "weeping prophet?" That's because he cried for Judah and Israel's sinful ways.

THE TREASURE IS FOUND!

2 Kings 22–23
622 B.C.

It was the eighteenth year of King Josiah's rule over Judah. Jeremiah was still speaking God's message of doom to Judah. And King Josiah commanded that the Temple of God in Jerusalem be repaired. He told the Levites to take the money brought to the Temple to buy supplies and pay the workers.

626 B.C.	621 B.C.	601 B.C.
JEREMIAH CRIES	JOSIAH FINDS THE BOOK OF THE LAW	DANIEL'S CAPTIVITY IN BABYLON

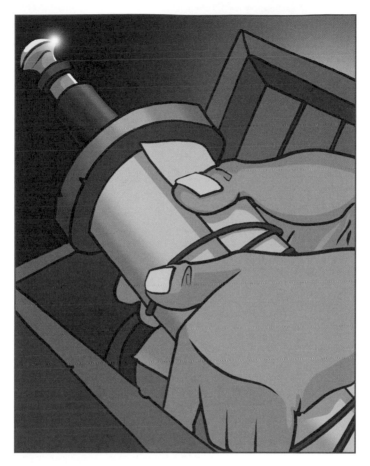

BOOK OF
THE TEACHING

    While they were bringing the money out of the Temple,
Hilkiah the priest found the long- lost Book of the Teachings

• **Syria, Palestine.** Scythian raiders attacked these two countries.

• **620 B.C. Greece.** Scribes wrote Greek laws in stone in public places for all the people to read. These were done in the busiest parts of the cities so the most people would see them.

• **Greece.** Good elementary education was being offered in Nubia.

• **Judah.** The Book of the Teachings of God were found in the Temple in Jerusalem after having been lost for decades.

• **Egypt.** Necho II, King of Egypt, started building a canal between the Nile River and the Red Sea.

of the Lord that had been given to Moses. What a treasure! Hilkiah gave the Book to Shaphan, the royal assistant, who read it.

Then Shaphan went to see King Josiah and said, "Hilkiah the priest has given me a book." And Shaphan read from the Book to the king. When the king heard God's words from the Book of the Teachings, he knew it was God's holy words and that Judah had not obeyed them. So he tore his clothes to show how upset he was.

King Josiah sent Shaphan and some other men to ask the Lord about the words in the Book of the Teachings. So Shaphan, his son Ahikam, Acbor, and Asaiah went to see Huldah, a prophet of God. They asked her what the Lord's words meant.

Huldah told the men that God was angry with Judah for worshiping other gods and not following his words. She said that he was going to bring trouble to Judah, and that his anger could not be stopped. She also said that God had seen Josiah's sadness because Judah had not obeyed him. And God would let Josiah die, rather than have to watch Jerusalem and Judah be

destroyed. And that's the message that Shaphan and the others took back to King Josiah.

THE PEOPLE HEAR THE TEACHINGS

When King Josiah heard what God had said, he gathered all the people of Judah at the Temple of the Lord. There he read to them all the words of God from the Book of the Teachings. Then King Josiah made a solemn promise to God that he would obey all the Teachings of the Book. And the people promised to obey them, too.

After that, King Josiah destroyed everything in all the land that honored any god except the God of heaven. He destroyed their places of worship to false gods, their false priests and prophets, their idols, their places of sacrifice, their fortune-tellers and witches, and anything else that had to do with the evil they had begun to do.

Finally, King Josiah commanded the people to celebrate the Passover feast—the feast God began when he rescued Israel from slavery in Egypt.

The Bible says, "There was no king like Josiah before or after him. He obeyed the Lord with all his heart, soul and strength. He followed all the Teachings of Moses."

DID YOU KNOW...

Josiah was king for 31 long years, but when he died in battle, he was still only 39 years old?

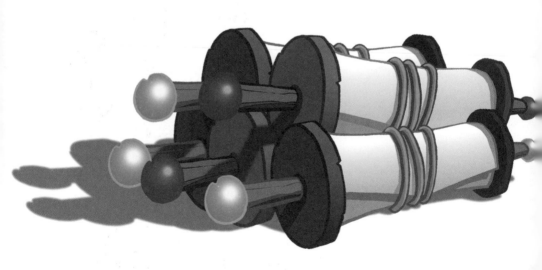

DANIEL AND THE DREAM

Daniel 1–2 • 601 B.C.

A price always has to be paid for sin. King Josiah had brought Judah back to God, but the people still had to pay the price for the horrible sins they had done earlier under Manasseh. And the time for them to pay the price had come, just as Jeremiah the prophet had said it would.

621 B.C.	601 B.C.	597 B.C.
JOSIAH FINDS THE BOOK OF THE LAW	DANIEL'S CAPTIVITY IN BABYLON	GREAT DEPORTATION

TAKEN CAPTIVE!

Egypt and Babylon had one of the worst battles in history. Babylon defeated Egypt and then took Judah captive. Many people from Judah, including a young man named Daniel, were taken to Babylon as slaves. Soon several young men from Judah were chosen for special service in King Nebuchadnezzar's palace. One of those men was Daniel, along with his friends Shadrach, Meshach, and Abednego.

THE KING'S DREAM

One night King Nebuchadnezzar had a dream. The dream troubled the king, and he couldn't sleep. So he called for his wise men to come and tell him what the dream meant.

The wise men said, "Tell us your dream, O King, and we will tell you what it means."

But the king said, "No. You must tell me what dream I dreamed and what it means. Or you will die."

But the wise men could not tell the king what dream he had dreamed. So Nebuchadnezzar had them all killed.

Then Daniel came to see the king. God helped Daniel tell the king what dream he had dreamed and what it meant. He said

that the king had dreamed about a huge statue that was made of gold, silver, bronze, iron, and clay. He explained that each of

those metals stood for a kingdom that would rule in the future.

Then he said that the king had dreamed that a rock was thrown at the feet of the statue, the statue was broken into pieces, and the wind blew it away. Daniel said that meant that God would send a kingdom someday that would destroy all the other kingdoms, but God's kingdom would never be destroyed. (He was talking about the kingdom of Jesus!)

DANIEL REWARDED

The king was amazed! He fell down on his face in front of Daniel and praised God. Then the king put Daniel in an important job in Babylon. He became ruler over all of Babylon, and he was put in charge of all the wise men. The king also appointed Shadrach, Meshach, and Abednego to be rulers over the land under Daniel.

Nebuchadnezzar was amazed at what Daniel's God could do, but he didn't totally believe in God. And he didn't stop making Judah serve him as slaves.

DID YOU KNOW...

Daniel's Babylonian name was Belteshazzar? They made him change his Hebrew name when he was taken captive.

• **Mexico.** The Mayan civilization existed.

• **605** B.C. **Judah.** The Bible prophet, Jeremiah, dictated his prophecies of twenty-three years to his secretary, Baruch.

• **600** B.C. **Greece.** Greek art became independent from other cultures. Their architecture changed from the hard lines of the Doric style to the softer, more graceful lines of the Ionic style of art.

• **Greece.** Pythagoras invented the eight-note octave. They also watered with artificial irrigation.

• **Chios.** An inventor named Glaucus introduced the process of soldering iron.

DEPORTED TO BABYLON
Jeremiah 36
2 Kings 24 • 597 B.C.

*A*fter good King Josiah
died, his son Jehoahaz
ruled for a short time. Then Josiah's
son Jehoiakim became king of Judah.
Jehoiakim was not good like his father, and
he brought false gods back into Judah. So
Jeremiah the prophet continued to warn
Judah about the coming captivity.

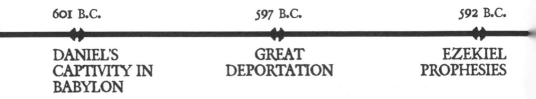

601 B.C.	597 B.C.	592 B.C.
DANIEL'S CAPTIVITY IN BABYLON	GREAT DEPORTATION	EZEKIEL PROPHESIES

JEREMIAH'S SCROLL

During Jehoiakim's rule, God told Jeremiah to write down all the prophecies he had spoken in the twenty-three years he had been delivering God's messages. So Jeremiah dictated all his past prophecies to his secretary—a man named Baruch. It was a long, hard job to prepare the scroll of Jeremiah's prophecies, and Baruch was happy when they were finished.

When the scroll was finished, Jeremiah told Baruch to take it

- **Corsica.** The Phoenicians invaded Corsica.

- **Greece.** Papyrus was first used as writing material.

- **Greece.** Alcman and Arion lived and wrote poetry and music.

- **597** B.C. **Judah.** Zedekiah, the last king of Judah, began his reign.

- **600-300** B.C. **Egypt.** Instruments for surveying land were invented. They invented the groma to set out squares and rectangles. This was a simple cross of wood held horizontally. Plumb lines hanging from each stick allowed surveyors to sight along lines at exact right angles.

to the Temple of God and read it out loud. Reading the scroll reminded the people of Judah of all the warnings they had received from God. Then Baruch read it to the king's officers. When they heard the words of God in the scroll, they were afraid. And they told Baruch and Jeremiah to hide from King Jehoiakim.

The officers read the scroll of Jeremiah to King Jehoiakim. But Jehoiakim did not listen to the words of God. Instead, he cut the scroll into pieces and burned it. And he told the officers to arrest Baruch and Jeremiah, but God had hidden them, and they could not be found.

After that, God told Jeremiah to dictate all his prophecies to Baruch again. So they prepared a second scroll, which was kept safe from Jehoiakim.

DEPORTED!

After Babylon took Judah captive, King Jehoiakim died, and his son Jehoiachin became king. But he only ruled for three months. Then King Nebuchadnezzar sent Jehoiachin away to Babylon as a captive, and he appointed King Josiah's third son, Zedekiah, as King of Judah.

It was at that time that many more people from Judah were deported from Judah to Babylon as captives. More people were deported this time than ever before or after. And one of the people deported was a man named Ezekiel.

DISCIPLINE AND LOVE

Once again God's words had come true. The people of Judah were being punished for the evil things they had done. God was punishing them because he loved them so much, and he wanted them to come back to him. It was just as wise King Solomon had once said: "The Lord corrects those he loves, just as a father corrects the child that he likes."

in the Bible there are about 773,692 words? That's about 3,566,480 letters! Imagine how tired Baruch would have been if he had written the whole Bible, instead of just the Book of Jeremiah.

DANCE OF THE DRY BONES

The Book of Ezekiel
592 B.C.

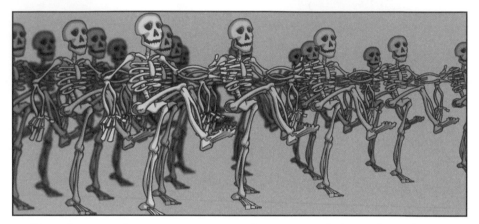

*G*od's people were separated. Many of them had been taken to Babylon as captives; the rest were still in Judah. During this time God had two prophets: Jeremiah and Ezekiel. Jeremiah continued to deliver God's messages to the people of Judah in Jerusalem, while Ezekiel began speaking to the people of Judah who were captives in Babylon.

597 B.C.	592 B.C.	588-586 B.C.
GREAT DEPORTATION	EZEKIEL PROPHESIES	BABYLONIA CAPTURES JERUSALEM

God spoke to Ezekiel in very unusual ways. Ezekiel often had strange dreams and saw visions from God. In these dreams God told Ezekiel what to say to the people. One of the most exciting dreams was about dry bones.

DREAM OF DRY BONES

Ezekiel dreamed that God took him to a valley that was full of bones. The bones were very dry. Then God asked Ezekiel, "Can these bones live?" And Ezekiel said that only God knew if the bones could live.

The Lord told Ezekiel to speak to the dry bones and tell them this: "I will cause breath to enter you. Then you will live. I will put muscles on you. I will put flesh on you. I will cover you with skin. Then I will put breath in you, and you will live. Then you will know that I am the Lord."

So Ezekiel began to speak the words of God to the dry bones. While he was speaking to them, Ezekiel heard a rattling noise. Then he saw the bones come together, and muscles started forming on the bones. Next, flesh grew, and skin covered the bones. But they were still not alive.

After that, God told Ezekiel to speak to the wind and say this: "Wind, breathe on these people who were killed so they can live again." And Ezekiel spoke to the wind as God had told him to do. Then breath came into the flesh-covered bones, and they came to life! They stood up on their feet. And when Ezekiel looked, the dry bones had become a large army of living people.

IN THE WORLD

- **594 B.C. Greece.** The Greek ruler, Solon, made many social changes in Athens.

- **Greece.** A poet named Thespis held the first public performance of his tragedy based on a hymn to Dionysus. This was the beginning of drama. Actors started being called "Thespians" after Thespis.

- The Book of Ezekiel in the Bible was probably written.

- **600 B.C. Austria.** The winch (or windlass) was discovered. The main purpose of the winch was to give workers more lifting power when hauling things up on a rope.

WHAT THE DRY BONES MEANT

Then God explained the dream to Ezekiel. He said that he was going to bring life back to Judah—the people he loved so much. And he would bring them out of captivity and back to their homeland. Then Judah would know that their return to Israel was a gift from God and that it wasn't because of anything or anybody else.

Ezekiel was an actor? Once he lay down on his left side for 390 days! He was acting out God's message that Jerusalem would be attacked.

(See Ezekiel 4:1-17.)

JERUSALEM DESROYED

Ezekiel 24–28 • Jeremiah 21–31, 37–38
2 Kings 25 • 588–586 B.C.

*D*uring the days of Ezekiel and Jeremiah, King Zedekiah of Judah made a big mistake. He turned against King Nebuchadnezzar of Babylon. When he did this, King Nebuchadnezzar brought his strong army and surrounded all the cities of Judah, including Jerusalem, the Holy City of God.

592 B.C.	588-586 B.C.	584 B.C.
EZEKIEL PROPHESIES	**BABYLONIA CAPTURES JERUSALEM**	**SHADRACH MESHACH ABEDNEGO**

SURROUNDED!

Nebuchadnezzar's army set up camp all around Jerusalem. Then they built seigeworks against the walls of the city. Seigeworks were ramps of dirt that led to the top of the city walls, like roads. The army could run up the ramps and over the walls to attack the city.

By surrounding the city, Babylon's army cut off all food from coming into Jerusalem. Before long, there was no food at all left in the city, and everyone was very hungry.

A BREAKTHROUGH

Then Babylon's army broke through one of the city walls. When that happened, King Zedekiah and his whole army ran out one of the city gates, trying to escape. They ran toward the Jordan Valley, but the Babylonian army chased them and caught

them in the plains of Jericho.

Zedekiah's army was scattered and could not fight back. So Babylon's army captured Zedekiah and took him to stand before King Nebuchadnezzar. The king made Zedekiah watch as they killed his sons. Then they put out Zedekiah's eyes so that his sons' deaths were the last thing he ever saw. Finally, they put bronze chains on Zedekiah and took him to Babylon as a slave.

JERUSALEM DESTROYED

Nebuzaradan, commander of Nebuchadnezzar's special guards, went to Jerusalem and set fire to the Temple of God and the king's palace. He also burned all the houses and every important building in Jerusalem.

IN THE WORLD

- **589 B.C. Judah.** King Zedekiah rebelled against King Nebuchadnezzar of Babylon. This set off Babylon's attack on Jerusalem and, eventually, the complete destruction of the Holy City.

- The Bible Books of Lamentations and Obadiah were probably written.

- **586 B.C. Judah.** The Temple of God and Solomon's Great Palace were burned in Jerusalem by the Babylonian army.

- **Babylon.** The people of Judah began their slavery in Babylon.

- **Burma.** The Shwe Dagon Pagoda, a very beautiful oriental building, was built.

The Babylonian army broke down all the walls around Jerusalem and took the people of Jerusalem captive. But they left behind some of the poorest people of Judah to take care of the vineyards and fields.

Babylonian soldiers also took all the beautiful things used for service to God in the Temple and carried them back to Babylon. They took everything made of gold, silver, and bronze.

The Holy City of God—the City of David—had fallen to

Babylon...and its fall was very great. The prophecies of
Jeremiah, Ezekiel, and the other prophets had come true. And
yet, through it all, God loved his people and wanted them to
come back to him with their hearts. So, soon he would show
them a way out.

DID YOU KNOW...

there was so much bronze in the Temple of God that it couldn't even be weighed!

(See 2 Kings 25:16.)

FOUR MEN IN A FIRE

Daniel 3:1–30
584 B.C.

*B*ack in Babylon where the people of Judah were slaves,
Daniel was second in command to King Nebuchadnezzar
himself. When this story happened, Daniel was probably

away from the city on business for the king. If he had been
there, he surely would have tried to help his friends.

THE GOLDEN STATUE

King Nebuchadnezzar didn't really know or worship the true
God, even though he had seen God's power work when Daniel

told him his dream. So he had a huge golden statue set up near the city of Babylon.

Then the king called all the people together. He said that when they heard the sound of musical instruments, they were to bow down and worship the giant false god. If they did not worship the statue, they would be thrown into a blazing furnace!

Everyone bowed down to the statue except Shadrach, Meshach, and Abednego—the rulers of Babylon who served under Daniel. They would not bow down to any god except the true God of heaven.

DID YOU KNOW...

the gold statue King Nebuchadnezzar built was ninety feet tall and nine feet wide? **WOW!**

THE KING BECOMES ANGRY

King Nebuchadnezzar became angry! He ordered the furnace heated seven times hotter than usual. Then the three young men were tied up and thrown into the white-hot furnace.

THE ONE TRUE GOD

Suddenly the king saw something amazing. Four men, not three, were walking around in the fire! They were not tied up, and they were not even burned. The king had them brought out of the fiery furnace. Their clothes didn't even smell like smoke. It was fantastic!

IN THE WORLD

• **584 B.C.** A group of people in Judah ran away from the Babylonian army to Egypt. They forced Jeremiah the prophet and his secretary, Baruch, to go with them. They settled in the fortress city of Tahpanhes on the border.

• **Babylon.** While Nebuchadnezzar held God's people captive in Babylon, many books of the Old Testament, based on stories handed down by word of mouth, were first written down in the language of Hebrew.

• **Babylon.** King Nebuchadnezzar built the famous Hanging Gardens in the palace at Babylon. These gardens are one of the Seven Wonders of the World.

King Nebuchadnezzar said, "Praise the God of Shadrach, Meshach, and Abednego. Their God has sent his angel to save them from the fire!"

Then the king made a new law that said no one could speak against God because, he said, "No other god can save his people like this God."

Once again, King Nebuchadnezzar was shown the mighty power of God. But once again, he did not really believe in God or follow him. Someday, though, if the king continued seeing God's awesome power in action, he might really believe in God with all his heart.

THE GREAT TEMPLE DREAM

The Book of Lamentations • Ezekiel 40–48
572 B.C.

*J*eremiah had been right. Jerusalem was destroyed. Should he laugh and say, "I told you so?" No. Jeremiah was heartbroken that his city and his people were shamed and separated. His family and friends had been taken away to Babylon as captives. His hometown of Jerusalem was a pile of rubble. And even he was in a foreign country.

So, once again, this great prophet of God cried for Judah. He wrote of his sadness in a beautiful poem. His sad thoughts are called "laments." You can read Jeremiah's poem in the Book of Lamentations in your Bible.

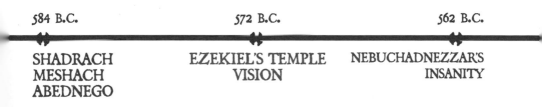

584 B.C.	572 B.C.	562 B.C.
SHADRACH MESHACH ABEDNEGO	EZEKIEL'S TEMPLE VISION	NEBUCHADNEZZAR'S INSANITY

FROM DESPAIR TO HOPE

Meanwhile, back in Babylon, the prophet Ezekiel was still with the people of Judah in slavery. When the news arrived about the Fall of Jerusalem, Ezekiel's message from God changed from despair to hope. He began telling the people that

God was going to gather up his people from the places they had been taken and return them to the Promised Land—Canaan, which was later called Palestine. He also reminded them that God was still planning to send the Messiah, the Savior, to rescue them one day.

IN THE WORLD

- **570 B.C. Egypt.** Ahmose II became king.

- **585-572 B.C. Phoenicia.** The city of Tyre was surrounded by the Babylonian army for thirteen years before it surrendered. When that happened, Phoenicia stopped being a nation forever.

- **580-542 B.C. Greece.** A famous Greek poet named Anacreon lived and wrote.

- **581-497 B.C.** The famous philosopher and mathematician, Pythagoras, lived and worked.

- **570 B.C. Greece.** A painter named Cleitias began using the Black Figure style of vase painting.

THE NEW TEMPLE

About twelve years later, God gave Ezekiel another amazing dream. He showed him a grand new temple. God showed Ezekiel all the details of the new temple, just as he had once described the Holy Tent built in the desert and Solomon's Temple that had recently been destroyed in Jerusalem.

Although some things about the new temple were to be like the first two, many things about the new one were to be different. Ezekiel's dream showed a man of bronze measuring the new temple. His measurements showed that the new temple would be much larger than the old one, and that was good news. But a much larger temple meant that it would take a lot longer to build, and that was sad news to the people in slavery.

God showed Ezekiel that there would also be some changes in the way he wanted his people to worship him in the new temple. He didn't want them just to follow his rules with their hands. He wanted the people he loved to worship him with pure hearts. He wanted them to live according to his commands and to obey them out of love for him, just as he wants us to do today.

DID YOU KNOW...

Greek philosophers at this time thought the Earth was a flat disk (like a plate) and it was covered with a dome of sky? They didn't know they could go "around the world" as we do.

NEBUCHADNEZZAR BELIEVES IN GOD

Daniel 4 • 562 B.C.

*D*uring his years as king of Babylon, Nebuchadnezzar had seen God's mighty power at work several times. The first time was when God helped Daniel tell the king his dream and what it meant. (See "Daniel and the Dream" on page 167). The second time was when Shadrach, Meshach, and Abednego were saved from the fiery furnace by an angel of God. (See "Four Men in a Fire" on page 193).

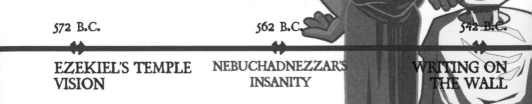

572 B.C.

EZEKIEL'S TEMPLE VISION

562 B.C.

NEBUCHADNEZZAR'S INSANITY

542 B.C.

WRITING ON THE WALL

Still, Nebuchadnezzar did not really believe in God as the only God of heaven. He continued to worship his other false gods, too... until something really strange happened to him.

THE KING'S DREAM

One night Nebuchadnezzar was sleeping when he had a scary dream. So he called for the wise men and fortune-tellers of Babylon to come and explain it to him. Just as before, Daniel was the only one who could explain its meaning.

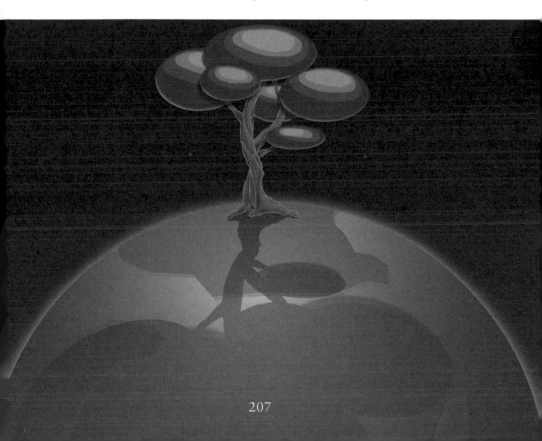

IN THE WORLD

• **561 B.C. Greece.** *Peisistratos became the tyrant ruler of the city of Athens.*

• **569-526 B.C. Egypt.** *King Amasis II was a great lover of music, drama, and the arts. He gave a lot of money to help develop them.*

• **550 B.C.** *The first five Books of the Bible, called the "Pentateuch," were clearly accepted as the Word of God or "Scriptures."*

• **550 B.C.** *The Bible Books of 1 Kings and 2 Kings were revised and finished.*

• **550 B.C.** *Pythagoras developed his math theorem that explained the size relationship of the sides of a right triangle.*

The king's dream was about a tree that was so large it could be seen from all over the world. Then an angel told him to cut down the tree, cut off its branches, strip off its leaves, and scatter its fruit around. But he was supposed to leave the tree stump and its roots in the ground.

Daniel told Nebuchadnezzar that the tree in the dream stood for the king himself. And God had told him that what happened to the tree was going to happen to the king. He would be forced away from people. He would live among the wild animals, and he would even think as an animal thinks. But when that time was finished, God said that King Nebuchadnezzar's kingdom would be given back to him.

THE DREAM CAME TRUE

One day Nebuchadnezzar was walking around on his roof. He might have been walking through the beautiful Hanging Gardens that he had built on his roof. He was thinking to himself how great a king he was and what wonderful things he had done as king. Then God spoke to him and told him that his dream was going to come true.

Right away, Nebuchadnezzar was forced away from people. He ate grass like an ox. His mind began thinking as an animal's does. His hair grew long like the feathers of an eagle. His fingernails grew long like the claws of a bird. And he stayed that way for seven years.

DID YOU KNOW...

the Bible is not the only record of King Nebuchadnezzar's temporary insanity? It is also reported in the Books of History of Babylon.

At last the time was over. The king looked up to heaven, and his thinking was right again. Then he praised God as the Most High God. He gave honor and glory to him. Then God gave the king back his kingdom, and he became even greater than before.

Nebuchadnezzar wrote a long letter telling everyone that God is the only God to worship and serve. And he sent the letter to all the people in all the world. Finally, Nebuchadnezzar really believed in God!

THE FINGER OF GOD

The Book of Job
Daniel 5 • 542 B.C.

*K*ing Nebuchadnezzar finally believed in God near the end of his reign. After he died, several other kings ruled over Babylon for short times. At last, King Belshazzar began to rule.

During this same time, the prophets Jeremiah and Ezekiel both died. And one of the kings of Babylon, named Evil-Merodach, released King Jehoiachin of Judah from prison and gave him back his place as an honored king. Meanwhile, Daniel continued to live and prophesy in Babylon.

562 B.C.	542 B.C.	541 B.C.
NEBUCHADNEZZAR'S INSANITY	WRITING ON THE WALL	DANIEL IN THE LIONS' DEN

JOB

It might have also been during these years that the story of a man named Job was written. The Book of Job tells how a good man was tested by Satan and lost everything he had, including his family. But after Job went through much suffering, God gave him back more than he had had before his troubles began. The story may have been written to give hope to the people of Judah, who were still suffering in slavery in Babylon. Some of those people had stayed faithful to God, but they had to suffer anyway.

DID YOU KNOW...

people began worshiping a false god called Buddha about this time? Today over 307 million people worship this false god.

BELSHAZZAR'S BANQUET

King Belshazzar was giving a large banquet. More than 1,000 people were there! During the party, Belshazzar had the beautiful things taken from the Temple of God in Jerusalem brought to him. Then he and his guests drank wine from them. But they praised their own false gods, instead of the God of heaven.

Suddenly a person's hand wrote words on the wall of the royal palace. Belshazzar watched the hand as it wrote. And he was terrified! His face turned white with fear, and his knees knocked together. He couldn't even stand up because his legs were too weak.

Belshazzar called for the

IN THE WORLD

· **550 B.C. Persia.** Cyrus the Great conquered the Medes and founded the Persian Empire.

· **547 B.C. Lydia.** Cyrus the Great defeated King Croesus and captured the capital city of Sardis.

· China's rival states are combined under Shih Huang Ti—the first emporer of China.

· **550-460 B.C. Sicily.** Epicharmus of Megara wrote some of the first comedy plays.

· **560-480 B.C. India.** The religion of Buddha was founded by a young prince named Siddhartha Gautama.

· **Greece.** The first water system was developed in the city of Athens. It had nine pipes that led to the main water well.

magicians and wise men to come and tell him what the strange words were and what they meant. But they could not read the words. Then Daniel was brought to the king.

Daniel said the words were these:

Mene, mene, tekel, parsin.

And he told the king that the words meant this: "*Mene*: God has counted the days until your kingdom will end. *Tekel*: You have been weighed on the scales and found not good enough. *Parsin*: Your kingdom is being divided between the Medes and the Persians."

Belshazzar rewarded Daniel with a royal robe, a gold chain, and he made him the third highest ruler in all of Babylon. But that night, just as God had said through Daniel, Belshazzar was killed. He had worshiped false gods. He had not worshiped the God of heaven. And his kingdom was taken away from him.

GOD SAVES DANIEL FROM LIONS

Daniel 6 • 541 B.C.

Who killed Belshazzar? No one really knows for sure, but it might have been Darius the Mede. God had written on the wall that Belshazzar's kingdom would be divided between the Medes and the Persians. And Darius the Mede became ruler of Babylon when Belshazzar died.

542 B.C.	541 B.C.	538 B.C.
WRITING ON THE WALL	DANIEL IN THE LIONS' DEN	RETURN TO JERUSALEM

A PLOT
AGAINST DANIEL

Darius liked Daniel and appointed him as one of three supervisors over Babylon. Before long, Daniel had done such a good job that Darius was planning to make Daniel ruler over all of Babylon. The other supervisors and governors didn't want Daniel to be promoted. So they tried to find something bad

IN THE WORLD

- **Babylon**. The Book of Daniel in the Bible was probably written.

- **Greece**. Public libraries were built in Athens.

- **550 B.C. China.** Lao-tzu founded the false religion of Taoism. Tao means "the Way" to happiness. Lao-tzu believed people should lead simple and natural lives in harmony with nature. By understanding nature's way, he said people could achieve inner peace.

- **550-510 B.C. Greece.** Travelers' maps were first drawn of large land areas by Anaximander.

about Daniel to tell the king. But they couldn't find anything bad about Daniel. He was trustworthy. He was not lazy and didn't cheat the king. But finally, they thought of a plan.

The supervisors and governors went to see King Darius. They talked him into making a new law that no one could pray to any god except Darius for thirty days. If they did, they would be put into a den of lions. In those days, a law made by the king could not be changed—not even by the king himself.

DANIEL PRAYED ANYWAY

When Daniel heard about the new law, he went home, opened the window toward Jerusalem, and

prayed to God, just as he had always done. He kept on doing this three times every day.

So the supervisors and governors went to King Darius and told him what Daniel was doing. They reminded Darius about the law he had made and said Daniel should be put into the lions' den. This upset Darius very much. He tried all day to think of a way to save Daniel, but his law couldn't be changed. So, that night, Daniel was put into a deep pit of hungry lions. Darius said to Daniel, "May the God you serve all the time save you!"

GOD'S ANGEL

King Darius stayed up all night. He couldn't sleep because he was worried about Daniel. The next morning Darius went to the lions' den. He found Daniel alive and well. An angel of God had closed the mouths of the lions. Darius was very happy.

Then Darius had all the evil supervisors and governors thrown into the lions' den, and they were killed instantly. And he wrote a letter to everyone in Babylon telling them to worship the true God of heaven—the God of Daniel who had saved him.

DID YOU KNOW...

in spite of what he had seen and said, Darius the Mede did not continue to worship God? Stay tuned to see what happened to him!

JUDAH RETURNS TO JERUSALEM

Ezra 1–2 • 538 B.C.

*T*he mighty empire of Babylon was growing weak and finally coming to an end. And Darius the Mede could see what was about to happen. But, instead of standing up for his people and being a man of honor, as Daniel was, Darius deserted Babylon. He became a traitor. He even

DANIEL IN THE
LIONS' DEN

RETURN TO
JERUSALEM

HAGGAI &
ZECHARIAH

helped Cyrus the Great, King of Persia, take over Babylon and become her king, too. After that, the Babylonians were never a powerful people again. And Babylonia became part of Persia.

THE KING'S ANNOUNCEMENT

Cyrus the Great was not like the kings of Babylon who had

ruled the people of Judah (now called "Jews") before him. In his very first year as king of Persia, he made an announcement to the Jews, who were still living there as slaves. He said that God had appointed him to rebuild the Temple in Jerusalem. And he announced that all the Jews were free to go back to Jerusalem to help build the Temple. They didn't have to go, but they could go if they wanted to. The Jews who stayed in Persia were told to help support the ones who would go to Jerusalem by giving them money, supplies, cattle, and special gifts for the Temple.

IN THE WORLD

- **539 B.C. Babylon.** Cyrus the Great led the Persians to conquer Babylon.

- **530 B.C. Persia.** Cyrus the Great was killed in battle.

- The Bible Books of 1 Chronicles and 2 Chronicles were probably written.

- **551–479 B.C. China.** The sayings of Confucius were collected into the famous work called Analects.

- **537 B.C. Persia.** Cyrus the Great freed the Jews and allowed them to return to their homeland.

- **Greece.** A Greek medical scientist named Alcmaeon from the city of Croton discovered the difference between veins and arteries in the human body.

DID YOU KNOW...

before Jerusalem was destroyed, Jeremiah predicted that the Jews would be captives for seventy years? (See Jeremiah 25:11-12 and 29:10.) It was exactly seventy years when they went back to Jerusalem!

GETTING READY

When they heard the king's announcement, the family leaders of the tribes of Judah and Benjamin got ready to go to Jerusalem. So did the priests and the Levites. They were going to Jerusalem to build the Temple of the Lord. God made all these people want to go. And all their neighbors helped them. Cyrus also helped by giving the Jews back the beautiful things that had been taken out of the Temple in Jerusalem by King Nebuchadnezzar when Jerusalem was destroyed. There were 5,400 pieces of gold and silver! Sheshbazzar, the prince of Judah, brought all these things along when the captives went to Jerusalem.

The total number of Jews who returned to Jerusalem was 42,360. This didn't count their servants and singers. They also took many horses, mules, camels, and donkeys with them.

BACK HOME

When the captives arrived at the site of the old Temple of the Lord, they made special offerings to help rebuild the Temple. They gave as much as they could. The Temple would be built again in the same place it had been before.

All the Jews settled in their hometowns. They were finally back home in the Promised Land, just as God had said they would be so long ago.

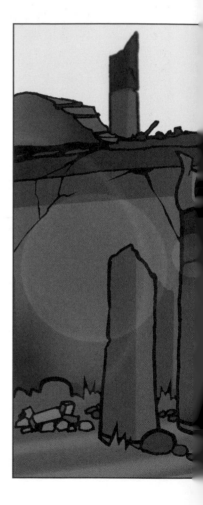

233

TROUBLE AT THE TEMPLE

Ezra 3–6 • The Books of
Haggai & Zecharia
520 B.C.

*T*he Jews were back in Jerusalem,
and work had begun on
rebuilding the Temple of the Lord.
They laid the foundation first, but
then the work stopped.

One reason the work stopped was
because the Jews' neighbors didn't
want the Temple rebuilt. So they tried
to stop the project. Another reason
the work stopped was because the
Jews were busy getting resettled in
the land. King Nebuchadnezzar's
armies had ruined Judah. The fields

538 B.C.	520 B.C.	516 B.C.
RETURN TO JERUSALEM	**HAGGAI & ZECHARIAH**	**NEW TEMPLE COMPLETE**

234

were full of weeds. The houses had been burned down. And the city buildings were all destroyed.

So the Jews had to work very hard rebuilding their own houses, planting crops, and repairing the destruction of the whole country of Judah. They didn't think they had time to work on the Temple of the Lord. They thought they would work on the Temple when everything else had been finished. But that was not what God wanted them to do.

GOD'S REMINDER

God sent two prophets to the Jews to remind them about the importance of building the Temple. These two prophets were named Haggai and Zechariah. Haggai preached sermons that reminded the people that building the Temple was more important than anything else they had to do. He told them to finish the Temple first, and then tend to their own houses and lands. He said that the reason they were having so much trouble was because they had made their own houses and lands more important than the house (Temple) of God.

Zechariah's messages were different than Haggai's. God sent Zechariah eight special dreams that gave the Jews hope for the future. Zechariah's message of hope was important because the Jews would have to wait hundreds of years before God acted again. Zechariah warned

• **522 B.C. Judah.** Zerubbabel was appointed governor of Judah. He and the Jews' high priest, Joshua, led a large group of Jews out of exile in Babylon and back to Jerusalem.

• **Judah.** The Bible books of Haggai and Zechariah were probably written.

• **520 B.C. Judah.** The foundation of the new Temple of God was laid.

• Jerusalem is still in ruins. The people are deeply discouraged.

• **520–447 B.C. Greece.** Pindar, a great composer and poet, lived and worked.

the Jews about the long wait they would have. And he told them about what would happen during those long years of waiting.

WORK IS
BEGUN AGAIN

The leaders and people of Judah listened to Haggai and Zechariah, and they began working on the Temple right away.

Then Haggai gave them a special promise from God. Because the Jews had listened to the two prophets and obeyed the Lord, he promised to bless them. And he did bless the Jews who were faithful to him during this time.

Zechariah's messages from God were important for two reasons. First, they gave the Jews hope for the future. Second, they showed that God's plan from the very beginning of time had not changed. He was still planning to send his Son Jesus into the world. And it was Jesus who would walk through this very Temple that the Jews were building. It was Jesus who would fill the Temple they were building with the glory of God himself. It was Jesus who would save the Jews and all of God's people in the world from their sins. God would send Jesus into the world because he loved his people so much.

DID YOU KNOW...

Zechariah placed a crown on Joshua, the high priest? This was a symbol that meant Jesus would someday be both high priest and king over his people. From that time on, the high priest was more like a king to the Jews.

THE NEW TEMPLE IS FINISHED

Ezra 6 • The Book of Zechariah
516 B.C.

*O*n March 12, 516 B.C., *the new Temple of the Lord in Jerusalem was finished. This was in the sixth year that Darius was king of Persia. The Jews were successful because they listened to the messages from God that came to them through Haggai and Zechariah. And they obeyed God's words.*

520 B.C.	516 B.C.	480 B.C.
HAGGAI & ZECHARIAH	NEW TEMPLE COMPLETE	ESTHER & MORDECAI

CELEBRATION!

Then the people of God celebrated. They gave the Temple to God to honor him. Everybody was happy! The priests, the Levites, and the rest of the Jews who had come back from slavery were excited. They weren't slaves anymore. They had their Promised Land back. They had their homes and families back together. And God had kept his promises.

This is how they gave the Temple to God. They offered these sacrifices to him: 100 bulls, 200 male sheep, and 400 male lambs. And as an offering to forgive the sins of all the nation of Israel, they offered 12 male goats—one for each of the 12 tribes of Israel. Then they put the priests and Levites into their separate groups. Each group had a certain time to serve God in the Temple at Jerusalem. This was all done just as it was commanded in the Book of Moses.

THE PASSOVER

Then the Jews who had returned from slavery in Babylon celebrated the Passover feast. They celebrated it just as the people of Israel had done when God led them out of slavery in Egypt so many years before. The priests and Levites made themselves

IN THE WORLD

- **507 B.C. Greece.** The form of government known as democracy was first set up in the city of Athens.

- **509 B.C. Rome.** The people of Rome set up a republic form of government.

- **516 B.C. Judah.** The new Temple of the Lord was finished in Jerusalem.

- **515 B.C. Persia.** King Darius built a splendid capital at the city of Persepolis.

- **582–497 B.C. Greece.** The philosopher, Pythagoras, used math to define pitches of the scale of notes. From this the Greeks began to write music, using letters of the alphabet to stand for the different musical pitches. We still use this system today.

clean, as God's law commanded. So they killed the Passover lambs for all the Jews who had returned from slavery, for their relatives, the priests, and for themselves.

So all the Jews who had come back from slavery ate the Passover lambs. So did those who had given up the unclean ways they had learned from non-Jewish neighbors. They worshiped the Lord, the God of Israel, the God of the Jews.

This was the greatest celebration the Jews had enjoyed in decades. And it went on for seven days! The Lord had made them happy. And they continued to praise him for the wonderful things he had done for them.

there were two kings of Persia named "Darius"? And there were two kings of Persia named "Xerxes."

LAST WORDS OF ZECHARIAH

After that, Zechariah gave his last messages from God to the Jews. Although it was still hundreds of years before Jesus would be born, God showed Zechariah important details about Jesus. So he tells the Jews that when Jesus comes, he will not be like the kings they've had in the past. He will not be a king of war, but he will be a king of peace. He will not come in riding in a chariot, but he will come riding a gentle donkey. He will be a loving king of the heart, just as God had always been to the Jews.

QUEEN ESTHER SAVES GOD'S PEOPLE

The Book of Esther • 480 B.C.

*A*bout forty years had passed since the new temple in Jerusalem had been finished. The Jews were still working to restore their country to what it had been before Babylon had ruined it. King Darius had died about three years before this chapter in the story of God's people happened. And a new King of Persia named Xerxes (ZERK-cees) was ruling.

516 B.C.	480 B.C.	465 B.C.
NEW TEMPLE COMPLETE	ESTHER & MORDECAI	MALACHI'S PROPHECY

THE PARTY

King Xerxes gave a huge banquet for all the important people in the whole Persian Empire. The banquet lasted 180 days! During the party Xerxes showed off all the wealth of his

kingdom and the splendor of his own kingship. One of the things he wanted to show off was his queen. So he sent for Queen Vashti to come to the banquet wearing her royal crown. But she would not go. (The reason Queen Vashti would not go to the king's party was because he might have been asking her to come wearing *only* the royal crown... and no clothes!) When she didn't come Xerxes became angry; so he took Vashti off the throne, and she was no longer queen.

THE CONTEST

Then all the pretty young women from all over Persia were brought to Xerxes so he could choose a new queen. He finally chose a beautiful young Jewish girl named Esther. And the king loved her very much.

- **480 B.C. Persia.** The Persian Wars began. The Greeks were defeated at Thermopylae.

- **490 B.C. Greece.** The Persian army was defeated by the Greeks on the Plain of Marathon.

- **490 B.C. Africa.** Hanno of the city of Carthage led an expedition of sixty ships down the west coast of Africa as far as Gambia. There they set up six cities.

- **Persia.** The Bible book of Esther was probably written.

- **Greece.** Great thinkers, Socrates and Plato, began the study of philosophy in Athens. Philosophy is still studied today.

THE PLOT

An important man named Haman hated the Jewish people. That was because Esther's uncle Mordecai would not bow down to Haman as he passed him on the street. So Haman tricked Xerxes into signing a law saying the Persians could kill all the Jews in the Persian Empire on a certain day. (Haman didn't know that Queen Esther was Mordecai's niece and a Jew.)

When Mordecai heard about the law, he sent a message to Esther, telling her to talk to King Xerxes and save the Jews. But the king had a law that no one was allowed to talk to him unless he called for them—not even the Queen. Anyone who disobeyed this law could be killed.

THE RESCUE

Queen Esther was very brave. So she went to see the king anyway. She said, "If I die, then I die." But because he loved her, Xerxes did not kill her. Instead, he offered to give her anything she wanted, up to half of his whole kingdom! When Esther told him about Haman's plot to kill her people, Xerxes became very angry. So he made another law that said the Jews could fight back if the Persians attacked them. Then he had

Haman hanged on the very gallows Haman had built for Esther's uncle Mordecai.

Brave Queen Esther had saved God's people from being destroyed. And every year after that, even up to today, the Jews have remembered the brave thing she did and how God rescued them by celebrating the Feast of Purim. It was a great day for the people of God.

the Book of Esther is the only book in the Bible that does not actually mention the name of God?

MALACHI: PROPHET OF HOPE

The Book of Malachi • 465 B.C.

A *lmost twenty years passed after Esther saved God's people from being killed by the Persians. During that time King Xerxes' kingdom was failing. He was running*

out of money. And, finally, in 465 B.C. King Xerxes was murdered in his own bedroom in the palace. After that, his younger son became king. He was called Artaxerxes I.

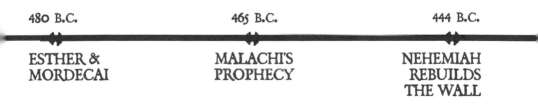

480 B.C.	465 B.C.	444 B.C.
ESTHER & MORDECAI	MALACHI'S PROPHECY	NEHEMIAH REBUILDS THE WALL

TIRED OF WAITING

Meanwhile, the Jews had continued to rebuild their country and the Holy City of Jerusalem. They were trying to make it as wonderful as it had once been. But they were getting tired of waiting for God to keep his promises about Jesus coming. They were tired of being ruled by Persia. They were starting to wonder again if God really cared about them or loved them. They had forgotten that the prophets Daniel and Zechariah had told them it would be a long wait.

The Jews had begun to wander away from God again, too. They had quit giving enough money to the Temple treasury to take care of the priests and Levites while they did their work. They had been offering sacrifices that were not pure. And the men had begun marrying women from foreign countries who worshiped false gods. So God was not happy with them.

DID YOU KNOW...

Malachi's name told people what his job was? It means "messenger."

MALACHI'S MESSAGE

Then God answered their questions and told them how sad he was about the way they had been living. He sent a prophet named Malachi to bring the Jews a message from him. And the very first thing God said through Malachi was "I love you." In spite of everything the Jews had done wrong, God still loved them. They were his people, and they still had a special job to do because Jesus had not come yet.

DAY OF THE LORD'S JUDGING

Malachi also told the people that a day would come when God would judge the people for the wrongs they had done. He said, "There is a day coming that will be like a hot furnace. All the proud and evil people will be like straw. On that day they will be completely burned up. But for you who honor me, goodness will shine on you like the sun. Then you will crush the wicked."

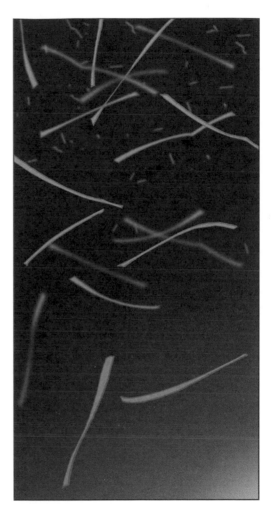

God was saying, "Don't give up, Israel! Hold on! The Messiah is still coming. I love you, and I will not forget my promises to you. Just be patient and wait a little longer."

IN THE WORLD

- **450 B.C. Rome.** The law code called the Twelve Tables was written and put into use.

- The Bible Book of Malachi was probably written.

- **450 B.C. Mediterranean countries.** The abacus was invented. It's an ancient type of calculating device. The first one was probably a dust-covered tray on which the person counted fingerprints. Later, the Chinese people invented the more modern abacus that has beads on rods. Today we use a calculator.

- **460–370 B.C. Greece.** Hippocrates, the Father of Modern Medicine, lived and taught.

REBUILDING THE WALLS OF
JERUSALEM

Ezra 7-10 • The Book of Nehemiah • 444 B.C.

*T*he Jews in Jerusalem had a long, hard task of rebuilding the Temple and the Holy City. The work was stopped many times by Israel's neighbors and enemies who didn't want Israel to become strong again. King Artaxerxes of Persia still supported them as they worked.

About 458 B.C. the great prophet and teacher of God's law named Ezra took fifteen hundred more Jews from Babylon back to Jerusalem to help with the rebuilding. It took them about five months to make the trip. But they took with them more treasures for the temple and the work of rebuilding.

When they arrived in Jerusalem, Ezra was sad to find that many men of Israel had married foreign wives. These women didn't believe in God, and they worshiped false gods. So Ezra told the men of Israel to divorce those foreign wives so they wouldn't begin following false gods, too. Many of them did as Ezra told them to do.

465 B.C.	444 B.C.	330-143 B.C.
MALACHI'S PROPHECY	NEHEMIAH REBUILDS THE WALL	MACCABEAN REVOLT; PERSIA FALLS

NEHEMIAH'S SADNESS

Back in the palace of King Artaxerxes in Babylon, about fourteen years after Ezra went to Jerusalem, news came to Nehemiah that Jerusalem's walls were broken down and her gates had been burned. Nehemiah was the king's cupbearer. (He protected the king by tasting anything served to the king before the king ate or drank it. He did this so that no one could poison the king.) The news made Nehemiah very sad. He cried for several days. And he prayed.

When the king saw how sad Nehemiah was, he appointed him governor over Jerusalem. And he sent Nehemiah to rebuild the walls and gates of the Holy City. When Nehemiah arrived in Jerusalem, he examined the wall to see what had to be done. Then he put the people of Judah to work on the wall.

Some of the workers rebuilt the city gates, while others worked on the wall. When they were attacked by their enemies, Nehemiah took half of the workers to guard the other half while they worked. And the Lord protected them.

WALL FINISHED

In only fifty-two days, the wall of Jerusalem was completely rebuilt, and all the gates were hung. Israel's enemies were shamed, and God's people were honored. Then Nehemiah led the people as they gave the walls and the gates to God, to honor him. After that, Ezra read the Law of God to all the people of

Israel, and the people made a new promise to worship God and only him.

The Holy City and her mighty wall were rebuilt. And the Jews once again worshiped and praised the God who loved and cared for them. It was one of the greatest days in the history of God's people. What a wonderful way for the Old Testament to end!

But still a greater day was coming, both for the Jews and for all the world!

DID YOU KNOW...

there are almost 400 years between the end of the Old Testament and the beginning of the New Testament?

IN THE WORLD

- **431–404** B.C. **Greece.** The Peloponnesian War raged between Sparta and Athens. Finally, Athens surrendered to Sparta. And a group of cruel rulers called The Thirty Tyrants were put into office.

- **Judah.** The Bible Books of Nehemiah and Ezra were probably written.

- **498–406** B.C. **Greece.** Sophocles was a leading playwright, who wrote Oedipus Rex. He also invented a writing style called the dramatic form.

- **444** B.C. **Judah.** The walls of Jerusalem were rebuilt under the leadership of Nehemiah.

THE NEW TESTAMENT

JESUS IS BORN

Matthew 2:2–10 • Luke 1:26–28 • Luke 2:1–20
6–3 B.C.

*T*he time had finally come. Everything that God had planned was in place. The eternal stage was set, and all the players were prepared to perform their assigned roles. God was ready to keep his promise to the Jews that he had made to Abraham over 2,000

years before. It was time for the Messiah to be born—the Son of God, the Savior of the world, the King of Kings and Lord of Lords, the Christ. And when the heavenly curtain went up, here's what happened.

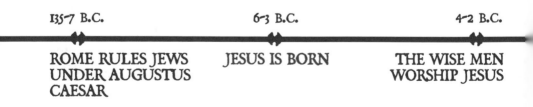

135–7 B.C.	6–3 B.C.	4–2 B.C.
ROME RULES JEWS UNDER AUGUSTUS CAESAR	JESUS IS BORN	THE WISE MEN WORSHIP JESUS

AN ANGEL'S MESSAGE

God sent an angel named Gabriel to visit a young woman who lived in the town of Nazareth in Galilee. Her name was Mary, and she was engaged to marry a man named Joseph. Joseph was from the family of King David of long ago.

The angel said to Mary, "Greetings! The Lord has blessed you and is with you."

But Mary didn't understand what the angel meant. So the

• **6 B.C. Judea.** The country of Judea and its people, the Jews, came under direct Roman control.

• **4 B.C. Judea.** Herod the Great, who killed all the Jewish baby boys under age two while trying to kill Jesus, died at age 69.

• **4 B.C. Judea.** John the Baptist was probably born.

• **Judea.** The Jewish religion had split into groups (called "sects" or "sections"), such as Pharisees, Sadducees, Essenes, Zealots, Herodians, and others.

• **3 B.C. Galilee.** A brilliant new star appeared in the eastern sky. Some scientists believe it was the one we call the Eastern Star.

angel said, "Don't be afraid, Mary, because God is pleased with you. Listen! You will have a baby boy, and you will name him Jesus. He will be great, and people will call him the Son of the Most High. He will rule over the people of God forever, because his kingdom will never end."

Mary said, "How will this happen? I'm not even married."

The angel said, "The Holy Spirit will come upon you, and the power of the Most High God will cover you. The baby will be holy. He will be called the Son of God."

Mary said, "I am the servant girl of the Lord. Let this happen to me as you say it will!" Then the angel went away.

THE BIRTH OF JESUS

Joseph and Mary had traveled to Bethlehem to list their names in a register as the emperor of Rome had commanded. While they were there, the time came for Jesus to be born. Since there were no rooms in the inn, Joseph and Mary stayed in a stable. And during the night, there in the straw, among the cattle, Jesus was born. It was the greatest moment in the history of all the world! And it happened in a barn.

it really took the wise men about six months to travel to where Jesus was? They didn't visit him in the stable. The Bible says they found him in a house.

(See Matthew 2:11)

SHEPHERDS WORSHIP JESUS

To announce his Son's birth, God sent a choir of angels to some shepherds who were taking care of their sheep in a field near Bethlehem. The shepherds hurried to the stable to worship the tiny king.

WISE MEN WORSHIP JESUS

God also put a bright new star in the eastern sky. And far, far away some wise men saw the star and knew that it was something very special. So they began traveling to where the star led them. The star was pointing the way to Jesus.

God had at last kept his wonderful promise. The Savior had come. But what would the world think of him? How would people treat him? Would they listen to him? And would they obey him? Only time would tell.

ESCAPE TO EGYPT

Matthew 2
3–1 B.C.

*A*fter Jesus was born, Joseph and Mary stayed with him in Bethlehem for several months. They moved from the

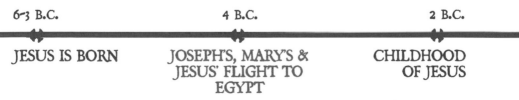

6–3 B.C.

JESUS IS BORN

4 B.C.

JOSEPH'S, MARY'S &
JESUS' FLIGHT TO
EGYPT

2 B.C.

CHILDHOOD
OF JESUS

stable to a house in Bethlehem. The news about the birth of the Messiah, who was also called the King of the Jews, spread quickly.

WISE MEN

The wise men had left their homeland about six months before this and finally arrived in Palestine where the star had led them. They probably thought, Who would know more about a new king of the Jews (Jesus) than the old king of the Jews (Herod)? So they went to see Herod at the palace in Jerusalem and asked him, "Where is the baby who was born to be the king of the Jews? We saw his star in the east. We came to worship him."

DID YOU KNOW...

the Bible doesn't say there were three wise men? No one knows how many wise men came to visit Jesus. We've always thought there were three because the Bible names three gifts that they brought.
(See Matthew 2:11.)

279

HEROD WAS AFRAID

When Herod the Great heard there was a new king of the Jews, he was very worried. The Roman Senate had given Herod the title King of the Jews, because he ruled over Palestine where the Jews lived. He was afraid that this new king would replace him. That's not what God had planned, but Herod didn't know it.

Herod asked the priests and teachers of the law where the Christ was to be born, according to Jewish teachings. They answered, "In the town of Bethlehem in Judea."

Then Herod had a secret meeting with the wise men. He

- **202 B.C.-A.D. 220. China.** The Han Dynasty ruled.

- **China.** Salt mining was developed.

- **1 B.C.** The people of Gaul began wearing Roman style clothes, such as togas. They also began shaving their beards.

- **North America.** Hunters in the southwest carried their hunting gear in animal-skin bags. These hunters belonged to the Anasazi people.

- **Rome.** Kitchens had metal saucepans and strainers, wooden spoons, and pottery pastry molds.

asked them the exact time they had first seen the star in the eastern sky, and they told him it had been about six months before. So he said to the wise men, "Go to Bethlehem and look carefully for the child. When you find him, come back and tell me. Then I can go worship him, too." (Herod didn't really want to worship Jesus; he wanted to kill him!)

As the wise men left the king, the star appeared in the sky to lead them again. They followed it to Bethlehem, and it stopped

over the house where Jesus was. After the wise men gave Jesus
wonderful gifts of gold and perfume and worshiped him,
they left.

ESCAPE TO EGYPT

Then an angel of
the Lord warned
Joseph in a dream to
take Mary and Jesus
to Egypt. He said to
stay in Egypt until the
angel told them to
return. So they got up
in the night and left
for Egypt.

HEROD'S PLOT

When Herod saw that the wise men had tricked him, he was very angry. So he gave an order to kill all the baby boys in Bethlehem who were two years old or younger. But God had protected his Son Jesus. And he lived to become the Savior of the world.

JESUS:
LOST AND FOUND
Matthew 2:19–23 • Luke 2:39–52 • A.D. 1–26

*A*fter Herod the Great died in *Judea, an angel of the Lord spoke to Joseph in a dream. The angel told Joseph to take Mary and Jesus back to their homeland because the people who were trying to kill Jesus had died. So Joseph and Mary took Jesus back to their own town of Nazareth in Galilee.*

There Jesus began to grow up. He became stronger and wiser, and God blessed him. The

4 B.C.	2 B.C.	A.D. 1-27
JOSEPH'S, MARY'S & JESUS' FLIGHT TO EGYPT	CHILDHOOD OF JESUS	JOHN THE BAPTIST

Bible doesn't tell us much about Jesus as a boy. The next time Jesus appeared in the Bible, he was twelve years old. And he was in Jerusalem with his parents celebrating the Jewish Passover feast. At age twelve Jesus had to begin learning the Law of Moses and obeying it. But Jesus understood the Law much better than other boys his age. And that's why an interesting story is told about Jesus at age twelve.

LOST!

When Mary and Joseph started home to Nazareth from the Passover feast in Jerusalem, they thought Jesus was with some of their relatives who were traveling with them. But Jesus had stayed behind in Jerusalem, and Mary and Joseph didn't know it. After they had traveled a whole day, they began looking for Jesus among their friends and family. But no one had seen him. Jesus was lost!

FOUND

Joseph and Mary hurried back to Jerusalem to find Jesus. They looked and looked for him for three whole days. They were surely very worried by that time. Finally, they found him at the

Temple. He was sitting with the religious teachers, listening to them teach and asking them questions. All the people who heard his questions and the answers he gave were amazed at how much he understood and how wise he was for his age.

When Joseph and Mary saw him, they were amazed too. Mary said, "Son, why did you do this to us? Your father and I were very worried about you. We have been looking for you everywhere."

Jesus asked, "Why did you have to look for me? You should have known that I would be here in the Temple where my Father's work is!" But they didn't really understand that he meant the work of God.

GROWING UP

Then Jesus went with Joseph and Mary home to Nazareth. He always obeyed them and did as they asked him to do. Jesus continued to learn more and more and to grow stronger. People liked him, and he pleased God.

Jesus stayed in Nazareth with his parents, his brothers, and his sisters. He worked as a carpenter with Joseph until he was about thirty years old.

DID YOU KNOW...

the age for a Jewish man to begin being a spiritual leader was age thirty? When Jesus reached that age, he began his work as a minister.

JESUS BEGINS HIS MINISTRY

Mark 1:9–11 • Luke 3:1–18 • A.D. 27

*A*bout six months before Jesus was born, a baby named John was also born. John was probably Jesus' cousin. And he had a very special job to do for God. His job was to announce to the world that Jesus, the Savior, had come. As this story opened, John was preaching in Judea. He was telling people that they should change their hearts and lives and be baptized. That's why he was called John the Baptizer or, more often, John the Baptist.

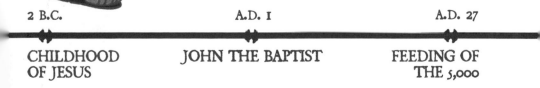

2 B.C.	A.D. I	A.D. 27
CHILDHOOD OF JESUS	JOHN THE BAPTIST	FEEDING OF THE 5,000

MAN FROM
THE DESERT

John was an exciting man to see and hear. He lived in the desert most of the time. He wore rough clothes made of camel's hair, and he had a leather belt around his waist. Many people from Judea and Jerusalem went out to listen to John. They told about the sins they had done, and then they were baptized by John in the Jordan River.

This is what John preached to the people: "There is one coming later who is greater than I am. I'm not good enough even to kneel down and untie his sandals. I baptize you with water, but the one who is coming will baptize you with the Holy Spirit and with fire." He was talking about Jesus!

Some of the people asked John what they should do to be right with God. John said, "If you have two shirts, share with the person who does not have one. If you have food, share that too."

To the tax collectors, who often cheated people, John said, "Don't take more taxes from people than you have been ordered to take." And to the soldiers John said, "Don't force people to give you money. Be satisfied with the pay you get."

DID YOU KNOW...

John the Baptist ate insects, called locusts, and wild honey as his food?
(See Mark 1:6.)

JESUS IS BAPTIZED

One day while John was preaching, Jesus came from his home in Nazareth to the Jordan River. He wanted John to baptize him. But John tried to stop Jesus. He said, "Why do you come to me to be baptized? I should be baptized by you!"

Jesus said, "Let it be this way for now, John. We should do all the things that are right." So John agreed to baptize Jesus.

After Jesus was baptized, he came up out of the river. At that very moment, heaven opened up, and Jesus saw God's Spirit, which looked like a dove, coming down on him. Then God's voice spoke from heaven and said, "This is my Son, and I love him. I am very pleased with him."

God will be pleased with us, too, if we change our hearts and lives and are baptized as he commanded.

IN THE WORLD

- A.D. **26–36. Judea.** Pontius Pilate was the Roman governor. He brought idols of the Roman emperor into Jerusalem, which made the Jews angry.

- A.D. **27. Judea.** Jesus was baptized by John the Baptist and began his ministry.

- A.D. **25–220. China.** Ways of producing food greatly improved. All these farming tools were invented: seed drills, better plows pulled by two oxen, harrows, grain mills, winnowing machines, and winch-and-pulley systems for irrigation.

- **Italy.** Romans were using two types of water wheels to grind corn.

- Fishing was a popular occupation.

THE MINISTRY OF JESUS

Matthew • Mark • Luke • John
A.D. 27–30

After Jesus was baptized, the Spirit of God sent him into the desert to be tempted by Satan. Satan tried hard to get Jesus to turn away from God, but Jesus avoided every temptation. He remained pure and holy.

Once his temptation was over, Jesus' preaching and teaching began. He traveled around the country to towns and villages to teach the people about God and about true worship. He did amazing miracles, and he told the people parables (stories with special meanings). The people loved Jesus, and many of them believed he was the Son of God and began following him.

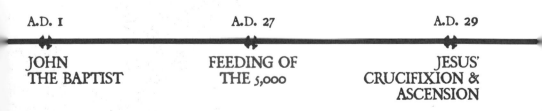

A.D. 1	A.D. 27	A.D. 29
JOHN THE BAPTIST	FEEDING OF THE 5,000	JESUS' CRUCIFIXION & ASCENSION

295

APOSTLES

Early in his ministry, Jesus chose twelve other men to help him take the message about him to the people. These men were called apostles. They were ordinary men, such as fishermen and tax collectors. But Jesus knew that each one of them had been chosen by God to be a special messenger, just as the prophets had been long ago. They stayed with Jesus wherever he went. They heard him preach and saw his miracles. They were eyewitnesses!

MIRACLES

Jesus did many miracles during his ministry. He made crippled people able to walk, he made blind people able to see, he made deaf people able to hear. Jesus helped sick people get well, he made evil spirits come out of people, and he even raised dead people back to life! There was no doubt about it—Jesus was the Son of God! No one else could do the miracles he did.

IN THE WORLD

• A.D. **28. Judea.** Jesus preached the Sermon on the Mount, including the famous Beatitudes.

• A.D. **28. Judea.** John the Baptist was beheaded by Herod Antipas.

• A.D. **20. Greece.** Strabo wrote his seventeen-book geography of all the world they knew about at that time.

• **North America.** Baby carriers were in use by the Anasazi people. They were made of light, bendable cradle boards padded with juniper bark, hides, or other soft material to cushion the baby's head. One of these baby carriers was found in Moqui Canyon, Utah, hundreds of years later.

TEACHINGS

The people loved to hear Jesus teach, because he taught with power. His words were strong and sometimes hard to live by, but the people knew he was telling them the truth. So thousands and thousands of them believed that he was God's Son and followed him. One of his most famous teachings is called the Sermon on the Mount. You can read it in your Bible in Matthew 5–7.

Jesus also taught with parables. These are stories that have special meanings. They helped the people understand what Jesus was preaching and teaching. You can read Jesus' parables in your Bible, too, in the Books of Matthew, Mark, and Luke.

Jesus used the words of the Bible to avoid Satan's temptations? And we can do the same thing today.

TROUBLE FOR JESUS

The leading priests and Pharisees became afraid of Jesus when so many thousands of people began following him. They thought he would take away their power over the Jews. So they began plotting a way to kill Jesus, even though he had done nothing wrong. They were planning something evil, but God was planning to use their evil for the good of the whole world. He was planning to give up the One (Jesus) he loved so much, for the ones (us) he loved so much.

THE SADDEST DAY

Matthew 23–26 • John 18–19
A.D. 30

*A*fter Jesus had preached for about three years, he went to Jerusalem to celebrate the Passover feast. When he came into town, thousands of people lined the streets to see him. They waved palm branches and shouted, "Hosanna!" (This word means "save now." They were asking Jesus to save them because they knew he was the Son of God.) So Jesus entered the Holy City as the King of Kings and Lord of Lords! Children sang. And the people bowed down and worshiped him. But this was to be Jesus' last journey.

A.D. 27	A.D. 29	A.D. 30
FEEDING OF THE 5,000	JESUS' CRUCIFIXION & ASCENSION	JESUS' RESURRECTION

THE LAST WEEK

During the next week in Jerusalem, Jesus often preached to the Pharisees and Sadducees about their evil ways. This made them angry, and they tried to think of a way to kill him. But they were afraid of what the people would do to them if they did. Then one of Jesus' own apostles, an evil man named Judas Iscariot, came to see the Jewish leaders. He offered to lie about Jesus so they could have him arrested and killed. They agreed to give him thirty pieces of silver for his lies.

ARRESTED

One day Jesus and the apostles had gone to a grove of olive trees called Gethsemane near Jerusalem. There Jesus went off by himself to pray. After he had prayed to God three different times, Judas Iscariot and some Roman soldiers came into the garden. And Jesus went out to

meet them. Judas came up to Jesus and kissed him on the cheek. That's how the soldiers knew which man was Jesus. Then they arrested him.

ON TRIAL

After that Jesus was put on trial several times. False witnesses, like Judas, told lies about him. And finally, Pontius Pilate, the governor of Judea, handed him over to be killed, even though he knew Jesus had done nothing wrong.

CRUCIFIED

On Friday, the Roman soldiers took Jesus outside of Jerusalem to a hill called Golgotha. And there they cruelly nailed his hands and feet to a big wooden cross. After a few horrible hours of hanging on the cross, Jesus died. When he died, God made the sun go black, and the whole world was dark for three hours in the middle of the day. One soldier said, "This man really was the Son of God!" And he was right.

IN THE WORLD

• A.D. *30*. **Rome.** *The city of Rome was the largest city in the western world with more than a million people living there.*

• A.D. *30*. *Jewish men wore talliths, which were prayer shawls. This was their way of showing that they were very religious.*

• A.D. *1–50*. *The Celtic people made bronze artwork and furniture. Shields, mirrors, daggers, and dagger holders were decorated with swirling art patterns and flowers.*

• A.D. *30*. **Rome.** *Chariot racing was a popular sport.*

BURIED

Later, a man named Joseph, from the town of Arimathea, took Jesus' body down from the cross and buried it in his own new tomb. Everyone thought that was the end. Jesus was dead and buried. He hadn't saved them from the Romans

as they had thought he would. And they began to wonder if he really was the Messiah after all.

But they were in for a great surprise!

the reason Jesus healed people was so that everyone would know for sure that he was the Son of God? Only God can perform miracles. These miracles also teach us that we can come to Jesus and ask him when we need help.

THE GOOD NEWS

Matthew 28 • Mark 16 • Luke 24 • John 20
Acts 1:6–11 • A.D. 30

*O*n Sunday morning, after Jesus was buried on Friday, a *miracle happened! Just as the sun was coming up, one of Jesus' followers named Mary Magdalene and another woman named Mary went to Jesus' tomb.*

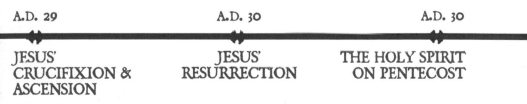

A.D. 29	A.D. 30	A.D. 30
JESUS' CRUCIFIXION & ASCENSION	JESUS' RESURRECTION	THE HOLY SPIRIT ON PENTECOST

THE ANGEL

Suddenly there was a strong earthquake! And an angel from heaven came down and rolled the stone away from the door of Jesus' tomb. He was shining as brightly as lightning. His clothes were as white as snow. The soldiers guarding the tomb were terrified of the angel.

DID YOU KNOW...

a Roman soldier was killed if he went to sleep on the job? That's why the story about Jesus' body being stolen while the soldiers were asleep was impossible.

HE'S ALIVE!

The angel said to the two Marys, "Don't be afraid. I know that you're looking for Jesus. He's not here anymore. He has come back to life! Go and tell his followers to meet him in Galilee."

The women left quickly to find the other followers. They were afraid, but they were so happy! Suddenly, Jesus met them and said, "Hello." The women came up to Jesus, bowed down, held his feet, and worshiped him. Then Jesus said, "Don't be afraid. Go and tell my brothers to go on to Galilee. They will see me there." So the women hurried away.

• **4 B.C.– A.D. 39. Galilee.** Herod Antipas governed Galilee. He was a good ruler for the Jews.

• **A.D. 30. Judea.** Christianity began when Jesus, the Christ, died, was buried, and came back to life. It has been followed by millions of people from then until now.

• **Greece, Rome.** Wine and expensive goods, such as bronze artworks, were traded to the Celtic people in Europe for cattle, skins, slaves, and salt.

• **Judea.** The Jewish people had many different kinds of baths. Some were for normal bathing, and others were for religious purposes.

THE COVER UP

The soldiers rushed into Jerusalem and told the leading priests everything that had happened. Then the priests and older Jewish leaders made a plan to cover up the truth. They told people that Jesus' followers had come during the night and had stolen Jesus' body while the soldiers were asleep. And that story is still told to Jewish people even today.

FOLLOWERS SEE JESUS

All the apostles, except Judas, met him in Galilee. Then he said to them, "All power in heaven and on earth has been given to me. So go and make followers of all people in the world. Baptize them in the name of the Father and the Son and the Holy Spirit. Teach them to obey everything I have told you. And I'll be with you all the way."

BACK TO HEAVEN

A few weeks later, Jesus knew it was time for him to go back to heaven. So he said, "The Holy Spirit will come to you. Then you will receive power from God. You will tell everyone the Good News about me in Jerusalem, then in Judea, in Samaria, and in every other part of the world."

Then Jesus was taken up into heaven, and a cloud hid him from their sight. Then two men wearing white clothes said, "He will come back in the same way you saw him go." So the followers went back to Jerusalem to wait for him.

CHRIST'S CHURCH BEGINS

Acts 2–5 • A.D. 30

*W*hen Jesus left the apostles and went back to heaven, he told them to wait in Jerusalem. The Holy Spirit was going to come and give them special power from God.

PENTECOST

About fifty days after the Passover when Jesus had died, another feast happened. It was called Pentecost, or the Feast of

A.D. 30	A.D. 30	A.D. 32-37
JESUS' RESURRECTION	THE HOLY SPIRIT ON PENTECOST	STEPHEN MARTYRED / SAUL CONVERTED

Weeks. It was a time for the Jews to give offerings of thanks to God for their good crops. Because Pentecost was one of the Jews' three most important yearly feasts, thousands of Jews came to Jerusalem to enjoy the feast together.

THE HOLY SPIRIT

During the celebration the apostles were all together in one place. Suddenly, they heard a noise that sounded like a strong wind blowing from heaven. This noise filled the whole house where they were sitting. Then they saw what looked like tiny flames of fire over each person there. When that happened, the Holy Spirit came into each one of them. He made them able to speak foreign languages that they had never studied.

Some religious Jews were staying in Jerusalem. They were from every country in the world. When they heard the noise that sounded like wind, a huge crowd came together. And they were amazed because all of them heard their own languages being spoken.

They said, "Aren't all these men (the apostles) that we hear speaking from Galilee? But they are speaking every language in the world. How can they do that? What does this mean?"

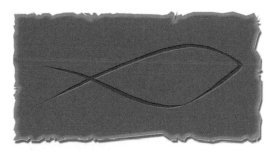

IN THE WORLD

• A.D. **31. Rome.** The Jews were allowed to return to Rome.

• A.D. **31. Italy.** Nero, the Roman emperor, was put to death at Pontia.

• The outline of a fish was a symbol for Christ. Legend says that the fish was a secret symbol during the times that Christians were being persecuted. When two strangers met, one would draw half of the fish in the sand with his foot. If the other person drew the other half of the fish, then they knew both of them were Christians.

• **Rome.** Ships had become the least costly way to trade goods with other countries. Roman trading ships were called "Corbitas."

THE GOOD NEWS

Then Peter stood up, and the other apostles stood up with him. He spoke to the crowd and told them the Good News about Jesus. Perhaps the other apostles repeated what he said in the other languages so all the people could understand; we don't know for sure. Peter said, "God has made Jesus both Lord and Christ. He is the man you nailed to the cross!"

When the people heard this, they were very sad. They asked the apostles, "What shall we do?"

Then the apostles told them, "Change your hearts and lives and be baptized, each one of you, in the name of Jesus Christ for the forgiveness of your sins." About 3,000 people that day believed what the apostles told them and were baptized.

BEGINNING OF THE CHURCH

After that the apostles did many miracles among the people. And everyone felt great respect for God. All the believers stayed together and shared everything they had. They ate together, laughed together, and loved each other. They praised God, and all the other people liked them.

Every day more and more people were being added to the group of believers, which was Christ's church. All the people who had heard the Good News in their own languages went home and told their own people about Jesus, too. So the church spread quickly through all the world... just as God had planned it all along.

DID YOU KNOW...

there were people from about seventeen different countries in Jerusalem for Pentecost? So the Good News was preached in seventeen languages that day!

(See Acts 2:5-12)

STEPHEN & SAUL

Acts 6–9
A.D. 32–37

*T*he Good News about Jesus spread *quickly through Jerusalem. So many people were becoming Christians that the Jewish leaders were afraid. But they couldn't attack the apostles without the people getting angry.*

DEACONS

To make certain that food was given fairly to all the Greek-speaking women whose husbands had died, the church chose seven men to take care of it. One of these special servants, called deacons, was named

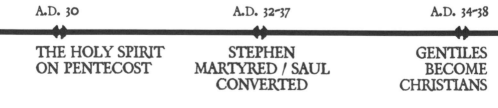

A.D. 30	A.D. 32-37	A.D. 34-38
THE HOLY SPIRIT ON PENTECOST	STEPHEN MARTYRED / SAUL CONVERTED	GENTILES BECOME CHRISTIANS

Stephen. The Bible says that Stephen was "a man with great faith and full of the Holy Spirit."

STEPHEN IS KILLED

Stephen was able to do great miracles. But some Jews were against him. They came and argued with Stephen. But the Spirit helped him to speak with much wisdom. His words were so strong that the Jews couldn't argue with him. So they paid men to tell lies about Stephen. The men said, "We heard him say things against Moses and against God!"

The high priest said to Stephen, "Are these things true?" Stephen reminded the Jewish leaders of how much God had loved and cared for them since the days of Moses. Then he blamed them for killing Jesus, the Messiah.

DID YOU KNOW...

Stephen was the first Christian martyr? A martyr is a person who chooses to die rather than give up what he believes. Stephen died rather than quit believing in Jesus.

When they heard this, they became very angry. They took Stephen outside the city and threw stones at him until he died. The men who stoned Stephen left their coats with a young man named Saul, who agreed to killing Stephen.

SAUL MEETS JESUS

Later, Saul was scaring Christians in Jerusalem by telling them he would kill them, too. Then he decided to go to Damascus to arrest Christians there also. On the way, a bright light from heaven suddenly flashed around him. Saul fell to the ground. A voice said, "Saul, Saul! Why are you trying to hurt me?"

Saul said, "Who are you, Lord?"

The voice said, "I am Jesus, the One you're trying to hurt." Then Jesus told Saul to go into Damascus and wait for someone to tell him what to do. But when Saul stood up to go, he was blind!

Saul's men led him into Damascus, and he waited three days. Finally, a Christian named Ananias was sent by God to see Saul. Then God made Saul able to see again. And he got up and was baptized right away. He became a Christian.

God had a special job for Saul to do, and soon Saul began to preach about Jesus in the synagogues. He bravely said, "Jesus is the Son of God!" Later we will see that Saul became the greatest preacher of all time.

NON-JEWS
BECOME CHRISTIANS
Acts 10 • A.D. 34–44

So far the Bible has been mostly about the Jews. People who are not Jewish are called Gentiles, or non-Jews. And now the Bible begins to tell us about them, too.

When God talked to Abraham hundreds of years before this, he had promised that all the nations of the world would be blessed through Abraham and his family, not just the Jews. God loves all people exactly the same—both Jews and non-Jews, as this story shows.

CORNELIUS HAS A DREAM

About three o'clock one afternoon a non-Jewish man named Cornelius had a dream from God. Cornelius was a Roman

A.D. 32-37	A.D. 34-38	A.D. 45-47
STEPHEN MARTYRED / SAUL CONVERTED	GENTILES BECOME CHRISTIANS	MISSIONARY JOURNEYS OF PAUL

officer of more than 100 men. He was a good man who gave many gifts to poor people, and he often prayed to God. God heard his prayers. So in the dream an angel of God told him to send for the apostle Peter, who was in the city of Joppa. Cornelius sent three of his men to Joppa right away.

PETER'S DREAM

About noon the next day, Peter went up on the housetop to pray, and God gave him a special dream, too. Peter dreamed about a big sheet coming down from heaven. It was full of all kinds of animals, reptiles, and birds. A voice said, "Get up, Peter. Kill and eat."

Under the Law of Moses, some of the creatures in the sheet were not supposed to be eaten by Jews. So Peter said, "No, Lord! I have never eaten food that is unholy or unclean."

But the voice said, "God has made these things clean. So

the word "Christian" means "belonging to Christ?" When you say, "I'm a Christian," you are really saying, "I belong to Christ."

don't call them unclean!" This happened three different times. Then the sheet went back into heaven. About that time, Cornelius' men came and asked for Peter. So Peter came down and went with them to the house of Cornelius in Caesarea.

NON-JEWISH CHRISTIANS

When Peter arrived at the house of Cornelius, many people were there. They wanted to hear what God was going to say to them. So Peter told them the Good News about Jesus. Then the Holy Spirit came down on all the non-Jewish people there, and they began to speak foreign languages. It was just like the day of Pentecost in Jerusalem.

That's how Peter knew that God was now offering salvation to non-Jewish people. That day Cornelius and everyone there were baptized and became Christians. And God kept his promise to Abraham to bless all nations through his family (Jesus). He blessed us that day, too!

• A.D. **41. Judea.** Agrippa was made king by Claudius.

• A.D. **43. England.** The city of London was founded.

• A.D. **43. Rome.** The Roman poet, Martial, was born.

• **China.** Weights and measures were set.

• **Jordan.** The desert temple, Petra, has some of the world's most amazing rock-cut architecture. It was cut out of sandstone cliffs. Petra was the capital city of the Nabataean kingdom. It's wealth came from trading goods with other countries.

ON THE ROAD WITH THE GOOD NEWS

Acts 13–28 • A.D. 45–60

*S*o that more people could be told the Good News about Jesus, the apostle Paul (Saul's new name) began to travel. He made three important journeys to many different cities and countries. There he preached and taught the people about the freedom Christians have as followers of Christ. He taught both Jews and non-Jews about the grace of God.

A.D. 34-38	A.D. 45-60	A.D. 61-64
GENTILES BECOME CHRISTIANS	MISSIONARY JOURNEYS OF PAUL	LETTERS TO CHURCHES

THE OLD LAW

While Paul was traveling, some trouble started between the Jewish and non-Jewish Christians. The Jewish Christians believed that the non-Jewish Christians should obey the Law of Moses, as well as follow Christ. After following the Law of Moses for hundreds of years, it was very hard for the Jews to think that it was no longer needed.

JERUSALEM COUNCIL

To settle the problem a meeting was held in Jerusalem. This meeting is known as the Jerusalem Council. The apostles and older Jewish leaders met to talk about the problem. After much talk, it was decided that the Jews should not make it hard for non-Jews to follow Christ. In other words, they agreed that the Law of Moses was not required for non-Jewish Christians.

GALATIANS

Shortly after the meeting in Jerusalem, Paul probably wrote the Book of Galatians. It was a letter from Paul to the Christians in the city of Galatia. In his letter he explained that Christians were not required to follow the Law of Moses anymore. He defended their freedom from the Law. He said that Christians had a new kind of agreement with God. And God had given them his wonderful grace.

TRAVELS CONTINUE

Paul traveled about for several years, preaching and teaching. During his travels Paul also wrote letters to many of the churches he had started. (We will talk about these letters in the next lesson.) Because Paul was popular among the people, the older Jewish leaders were jealous. So they began making trouble for Paul. Finally, he was arrested and put into jail.

PAUL'S TRIALS

Paul was asked to defend himself several times in front of different rulers and courts. Each time he told the truth about himself and about Jesus. In the end, Paul asked to be sent to Rome to tell his story to the Roman emperor, Caesar. As a citizen of Rome, Paul had that right.

While sailing to Rome, Paul's ship was torn apart by a storm that lasted two weeks. The shipwreck took place near the island of Malta. All the passengers got to shore safely because God

Paul wrote more of the books of the New Testament than any other writer?

saved them. They stayed on the island for three months, and Paul helped the people there. Then they sailed on to Rome on a different ship.

During Paul's journeys, thousands of people became Christians, and the church grew stronger everywhere he went.

IN THE WORLD

- A.D. **50. Germany.** The city of Cologne was founded.

- A.D. **54.** ROME. Nero became emperor when his mother, Agrippina II, poisoned Nero's father, Claudius.

- A.D. **47–120. Greece.** The famous historian, Plutarch, lived and recorded history.

- These Books of the Bible were probably written during this time: Matthew, Mark, John, Romans, 1 and 2 Corinthians, Galatians, Ephesians, Colossians, 1 and 2 Thessalonians, Philemon, James, and 1 Peter.

- The apostle Paul made three historic missionary journeys to preach the Good News of Jesus.

LETTERS TO THE CHURCHES

Romans • Philemon • A.D. 61–64

W hen Paul arrived in Rome, he was not taken to see Caesar. He was allowed to rent a small house and live by himself. He wasn't put into prison, but he was guarded by a Roman soldier. Paul lived there for two years.

During that time Paul was also allowed to have visitors and to preach and teach about Jesus. No one tried to stop him. So he invited many people to come to his house, and he spoke bravely about Jesus.

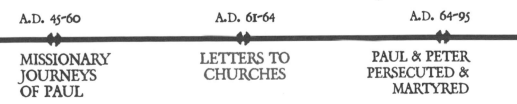

A.D. 45–60	A.D. 61–64	A.D. 64–95
MISSIONARY JOURNEYS OF PAUL	LETTERS TO CHURCHES	PAUL & PETER PERSECUTED & MARTYRED

WRITING LETTERS

During Paul's travels and his house arrest in Rome, he also wrote letters to the churches he had started during his travels. The four letters that he wrote while in Rome are sometimes called the Prison Epistles, because he wrote them while he was under house arrest.

SPECIAL LETTERS

Some of Paul's letters were written to special people, such as the Book of Philemon. Philemon had a slave named Onesimus, who had run away. Onesimus came to Rome, and there he met Paul. Paul taught Onesimus about Jesus, and Onesimus became a Christian. Then Paul sent him back to Philemon with the letter we call the Book of Philemon. In the letter Paul asked Philemon, a Christian, to take Onesimus back, not as a slave, but as a brother in Christ. The letter from Paul to Philemon teaches us today how to treat each other.

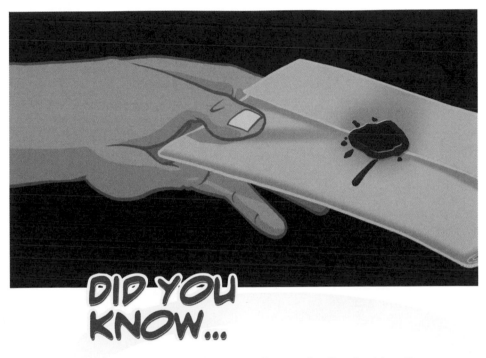

DID YOU KNOW...

the word epistle means "to send to"? The New Testament has twenty-one epistles, which is really just a big word for letters. You can write an epistle, too!

GENERAL LETTERS

Some of Paul's other letters were written to all the churches. In those days, a letter was read by one church. Then it was sent on to another church. Then to another, until all the churches had read it. Most people believe that the Book of Ephesians was a letter for all the churches. In that letter Paul showed how Jesus was the answer to God's promises and plans from the beginning of time. The letter also talked about a Christian's friendship with God.

MESSAGES OF THE LETTERS

Each letter that Paul wrote had a special purpose. Sometimes he wrote to help churches work out problems they were having, such as Philippians and Corinthians. Other times he wrote to teach someone how to do something. His letters to Timothy and Titus, who were preachers, were to help them know how to set up churches. Other letters were written to teach Christians how to live the right way.

Even though these letters were written hundreds of years ago, they are still our very best guide in how to live for Christ today.

PAUL, PETER, & PERSECUTION

Hebrews • Jude • A.D. 64–95

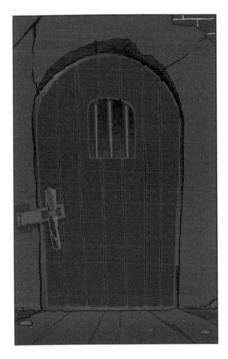

*F*rom the Bible and records of history, it seems that Paul was put into prison once again near the end of his life. Then he became a martyr for Christ. No one knows for sure how Paul died or where, but it's certain that he gave up his life rather than give up his belief in the Lord.

A.D. 61	A.D. 64	A.D. 95, 96
LETTERS TO CHURCHES	PAUL & PETER PERSECUTED & MARTYRED	REVELATION TO JOHN

NON-PAUL LETTERS

Not all the letters in the New Testament were written by Paul. Some were written by Peter, James, Jude, John, and others. From Peter's two letters (1 and 2 Peter), we can tell that Peter and Paul probably saw each other again in Rome. Peter also knew about Paul's letters and what they said. And, like Paul, Peter died as a Christian martyr.

PERSECUTION

About this time Christians began to be treated very badly. Some were whipped, some were stoned, some were killed by wild animals. Some were made to fight to the death against prisoners and slaves. Others were tortured by being left in the hot sun to burn to death. Some were drowned in boiling oil. Still others were thrown into prison and left to die. It was a very hard time for Christians. Some of the New Testament letters were written to give courage to the Christians who were being hurt.

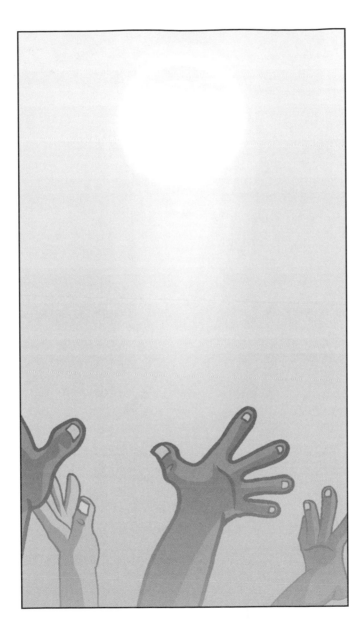

HEBREWS

The Book of Hebrews was a letter of courage for hurting Christians. Some of the Jews who were being persecuted for becoming Christians were turning back to the Law of Moses. Hebrews showed them how much better Christ was than the old law.

Who wrote the Book of Hebrews? No one knows for sure. Some people think it was Paul. Others think it might have been Luke or Barnabas or Apollos. But it's certain that the writer knew the pain and hurt the Christians were having to go through. So he reminded the Jewish Christians of all the great heroes of faith who had gone before them. He

IN THE WORLD

- A.D. **66. Judea.** The Jews began to revolt against Roman rule.

- A.D. **68. Rome.** Emperor Nero killed himself.

- A.D. **69. Rome.** Vespasian became emperor.

- A.D. **70. Judea.** Jerusalem was destroyed by the Roman army.

- A.D. **79. Italy.** On August 24 Mt. Vesuvius, a volcano, erupted. It buried the two Roman cities of Pompeii and Herculaneum.

- These Bible Books were probably written during this time: 2 Timothy, Hebrews, 2 Peter, 1 John, 2 John, 3 John, Jude, and Revelation.

- A.D. **67. Rome.** Peter and Paul, were both martyred.

talked about Noah, Abraham, and Enoch. And he told them to stay faithful to God, no matter what happened.

FALSE TEACHERS

The church was also having some problems with false teaching. People, who believed a teaching called the Gnostic philosophy, were telling false things to Christians in the church. So, some of the letters of the New Testament, such as 1 John, were written to help Christians avoid those false teachings. These were general letters that were passed around among the churches.

All these letters helped the early Christians to remember how very much God loved them. From the time of Adam and Eve until the time of Peter and Paul, God had never stopped loving and caring for his people. And he had not forgotten his promise to save them.

DID YOU KNOW...

the Christians dug long tunnels and rooms in the soft rock under the city of Rome? They used them to bury their dead and to hide. They also met in these rooms to worship. These underground passages are called catacombs. There are about 600 miles of catacombs under Rome!

THE FINAL VICTORY

The Book of Revelation • A.D. 95–96

*W*ith Peter and Paul both gone, leadership of the early Christians fell to one man—the old apostle John. But the Roman emperor, Domitian, put John in prison on the Isle of Patmos in A.D. 95. He thought that by taking John away the other Christians would soon give up their faith in Christ, and the church would die. John lived the

rest of his life on Patmos.

One Sunday John received a strange-but-wonderful dream from Jesus. An angel told John to write down everything he saw and to send it to seven churches in Asia. What John saw and wrote is what we call the Book of Revelation.

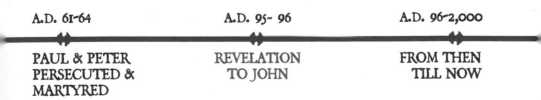

A.D. 61-64	A.D. 95- 96	A.D. 96-2,000
PAUL & PETER PERSECUTED & MARTYRED	REVELATION TO JOHN	FROM THEN TILL NOW

A CODED MESSAGE

The Revelation of John is a secret message, written in apocryphal (coded) language. It was written this way so that most Jewish Christians could understand it, but the Romans could not understand it. Then the Jewish Christians could tell the non-Jewish Christians what it meant.

At this time Christians were being attacked and hurt almost everywhere. They could not understand what had happened. Jesus had come and gone, but he had not rescued them from the Romans. Had Satan won the battle? Was the church going to be destroyed by evil? If not, when would God take charge? When would they be rescued? The Revelation was given to John to help answer these questions.

the word "revelation" means to "take the lid off" of something so you can look inside? God took the lid off his eternal plan to save us and let John look inside. Then John told us what he saw—victory!

THE MEANING

In John's amazing dream he saw God's plan from the
beginning of time unfold. It began with God as the great Creator
of the world—awesome and wonderful! Then he saw how
people had sinned against God and were forced out of the
Garden of Eden and away from God's presence. But God loved
people so much that he had made a plan to win them back to
him. That plan was to send his own Son, Jesus Christ, to save
people from their sins.

God chose the Jewish nation to be holy and good so that
Jesus could be born through them. Then John was reminded of
God's special law for the Jews given to Moses. And he saw how

God had taken care of his people all through the ages by sending them judges, kings, and prophets to bring them back to him.

Finally, John saw Jesus Christ himself, and he was dazzling! Jesus was fighting Satan's armies. And Jesus won the war! Satan was defeated, and Christians were brought to live with Jesus and God forever. Christians would have the final victory over evil.

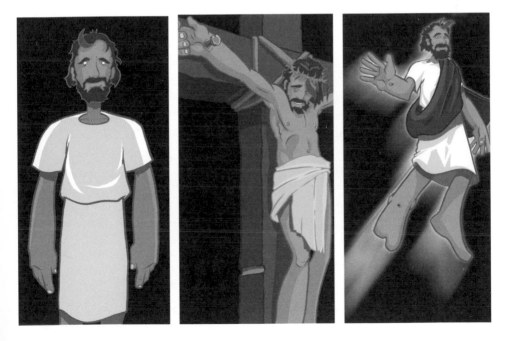

THE TRUTH

The dream that John saw is true. And someday, when Jesus comes back again, Christians will be taken to live in that wonderful city called heaven forever and ever. God has not forgotten his promise to save his people. We will have the final victory over Satan and evil. So we must pray, "Come soon, Lord Jesus!"

- **China.** Liquid ink was made by rubbing solid ink onto an inkstone with water. Then a brush was used to put the liquid ink on paper.

- A.D. **96. Patmos.** The Book of Revelation was probably written by Jesus Christ through John the apostle.

- A.D. **97. Ephesus.** Paul's traveling friend and a preacher, Timothy, became a martyr.

- A.D. **100.** The disease of pneumonia was first identified. No cure was found until about A.D. 1940.

- A.D. **100.** The disease of diabetes was first identified. No treatment was found until insulin was discovered in A.D. 1922.

GOD STILL LOVES US

A.D. 96–Now

*A*lmost two thousand years have passed since John saw
the revelation from heaven and the Bible was finished.
*That's about the same amount of time from the time of
Abraham to when Jesus was born. During that time many
exciting things have happened in the world. People have
lived and died. Rulers have reigned and fallen. Countries
have come and gone. Inventions have been built, and older
inventions have stopped being used.*

*In the last two thousand years, the world has changed a lot.
We have come from riding donkeys to driving cars, riding on
trains, flying in airplanes, and even traveling in spaceships to
the moon and back. We have come from writing on animal
skins, to typewriters, to computers, to sending messages all
over the world on the internet. We have moved from simple
outdoor amphitheaters to silent movies, "talkies,"
Technicolor, three-dimensional films, wrap-around sound,
and now to virtual reality computer programs.*

A.D. 95	A.D. 96	A.D. 2,000
REVELATION TO JOHN	FROM THEN. . .	. . .TILL NOW

GOD IS STILL THERE

Through all of these amazing changes, God has still been with us. When we are having hard times, God is with us, helping us get through them. He hears us when we pray to him, just as he heard Jesus and Paul and the apostles.

God is still in control of the world. He sets up governments, puts rulers in office, and guides the people who are at war. He is still taking care of the church, his special people in the world. He gives us courage and hope to go on. And he tells us through the Bible that we will be with him forever in heaven someday.

OUR JOB

Some things in the world have not changed. As Christians, we still have a special job to do, just as the Jews had a special job to do. Jesus told his apostles before he went back to heaven that he wanted his followers to tell people everywhere in the world the Good News about him. As his followers today we are now his prophets and teachers in the world. He has sent us to bring people back to him. We must tell our friends, our families, and our neighbors that God loves them, that God wants them to be his children, and that God wants them to live with him in heaven.

Just as Jesus died to save the Jews and the non-Jews of his time, he died to save us, too. As the Bible says in John 3:16, "God loved the world (us!) so much that he gave his only Son... so that whoever believes in him (us!) may not be lost, but have eternal life." Thank you, God, for your amazing gift of love, grace, and salvation.